The Soul-less Souls of Black Folk

A Sociological Reconsideration of Black Consciousness as Du Boisian Double Consciousness

Paul C. Mocombe

UNIVERSITY PRESS OF AMERICA,® INC.
Lanham • Boulder • New York • Toronto • Plymouth, UK

Copyright © 2009 by
University Press of America,® Inc.
4501 Forbes Boulevard
Suite 200
Lanham, Maryland 20706
UPA Acquisitions Department (301) 459-3366

Estover Road
Plymouth PL6 7PY
United Kingdom

All rights reserved
Printed in the United States of America
British Library Cataloging in Publication Information Available

Library of Congress Control Number: 2008936783
ISBN-13: 978-0-7618-4295-8 (paperback : alk. paper)
ISBN-10: 0-7618-4295-0 (paperback : alk. paper)
eISBN-13: 978-0-7618-4296-5
eISBN-10: 0-7618-4296-9

∞™ The paper used in this publication meets the minimum requirements of American National Standard for Information Sciences—Permanence of Paper for Printed Library Materials, ANSI/NISO Z39.48-1992.

Contents

Acknowledgments	v
1 Introduction to The Souls of Black Folk	1
2 A Structural Reading of African American History in America	19
3 On the Interpretation of Du Bois's Double Consciousness	46
4 Black Consciousness Today	71
References Cited	79
Index	93

Acknowledgments

The research for this work was conducted while the author was a graduate student in the Ph.D. in Comparative Studies, the Public Intellectuals Program at Florida Atlantic University. I am grateful to the faculty, fellow classmates, and staff for their intellectual stimulation and support throughout the years. Drafting of the manuscript took place mainly in the S.E. Wimberly library on the Boca Raton campus of the University, and at the new African American Research library in Fort Lauderdale, Florida. Members of the staff at both centers provided library facilities and administrative services that made possible the completion of the writing within its appointed time.

My analysis and conclusions are a result of the mentoring of two great professors, the late Drs. Stanford M. Lyman and Teresa Brennan. To them I owe my intellectual and theoretical growth and framework. Lastly, I would like to thank my grandparents, Saul and Eugenia Mocombe, my spiritual mother Corliss Ann Russell, and my wife, Tiara Mocombe, who taught me why and how to love.

Chapter One

Introduction to The Souls of Black Folk

In 1903 W.E.B. Du Bois in *The Souls of Black Folk* articulated what he thought to be the nature of black consciousness, which has shaped contemporary understanding of African American life. According to Du Bois, building on the bourgeois ideology of nationalism to account for the constitutive identity of the black nation living side by side with white American society, the black American has a "double-consciousness:" a "twoness" of being an American, and a Negro; "two warring ideals in one dark body, whose dogged strength alone keeps it from being torn asunder" (Du Bois, 1995 [1903]: 45). Through this conception Du Bois attempted to constitute the identity of the black American nation, and refute 19th century racial understanding of black life, which suggested that blacks were racially inferior to whites and had no culture or consciousness aside from that acquired through their contact with "whites."

Although Du Bois through "double-consciousness" attempted to define black identity and refute the inferior characterization of black American consciousness grounded in the fictitious ideology of 19th century racial science and biological determinism, as mediated by the concept of nation, the contemporary reliance on his construct to explain African American life, like Du Bois's position, is problematic.

Du Bois's position, the "doubleness" constitutive identity of the black nation, is grounded in the same racial science and the ideology of biological determinism he attempted to refute. This view assumes that while the American-ness of black American life was a result of their sociocultural contact with whites, the cultural ideas and practices associated with their "Negro-ness" was grounded in their biological determining racial type. Du Bois utilized the idea of race as a substance both biological and spiritual (the "souls" of black folk) to inscribe black folk in a temporal community, black nation, defined by its "doubleness," American and Negro.

Just the same, in spite of the cultural turn to understanding consciousness formation that dominates contemporary social science paradigms, the usage of Du Boisian "double-consciousness" by the so-called adaptive-vitality school also reiterates Du Bois's biological determining notion of "blackness" or "Negro-ness" to refute the social structural determinist position of the pathological-pathogenic school, which itself reiterates nineteenth-century conclusions regarding African-American life.

In order to better understand Du Bois's double consciousness as the ideological nature of black American consciousness, this work attempts to outline a theoretically meaningful thesis on the development and nature of black consciousness within the American capitalist bourgeois social structure. To this end, I develop a sociological model to explain the origins and nature of consciousness. I then subsume my sociological explanation in an historical narrative of the most significant event, slavery, in black life that helped constitute black consciousness. In the final analysis, I reinterpret W. E. B. Du Bois's double consciousness construct within the parameters of my sociological explanation and historical narrative.

The conclusion from these critiques is twofold. First, black American consciousness is not dual or bicultural, nor is the black community a "real" community, i.e., nation, defined by its "doubleness" or dual ethnicity. Black American consciousness is instead multiple and diverse, but dominated by the discursive practices of the liberal black (male) bourgeoisie which for a long time served as the bearers of ideological domination for the "black" community.[1]

Second, the autobiographical construct black double consciousness highlighted by Du Bois should be understood more in relation to the purposive rationality, i.e., the imaginary "fictive ethnicity," or "class racism," (Etienne Balibar's terms) of this particular group of the community, the black (male) bourgeoisie, (which, following the civil war, wanted equality of distribution and recognition with its white counterpart) than as an externally valid construct representing the duality of black American identity. In other words, Du Bois, as a member of this group, captures with the double consciousness construct their ambivalence toward American society; the desire of his class to obtain the liberal promises (equality of opportunity, distribution, and recognition) of American society against their derision for that same society because of its anti-liberal discriminatory practices against the black American. Hence deconstructed from its reliance on nineteenth century racial science and ideology, double consciousness is actually a reference to Du Bois's ambivalence toward American society rather than an accurate representation of black American consciousness in the bicultural sense.

THE DU BOISIAN DILEMMA

Published when W.E.B. Du Bois was thirty-five and working as an economics and history teacher at Atlanta University, *The Souls of Black Folk* is a collection of nine previously published essays and five new writings. The "double consciousness" construct with which the work commenced is formulated in the essay titled "Of Our Spiritual Strivings" from Du Bois's 1897 *Atlantic* magazine essay, "Strivings of the Negro People," published in the same year as his essay, "The Conservation of Races." The significance and relevance of the construct centers on whether or not it offers a sociohistorical understanding of black American self-identity or consciousness in the context of 19th century racial science and ideology that proposed that the black race or nation was inferior to whites and had no identity, culture, souls, or consciousness aside from that acquired through their contact with "whites."

According to Kirt H. Wilson:

> [s]ix years before *The Souls of Black Folk*, in an essay titled "The Conservation of Races" (1970, original work published in 1897), Du Bois offers the following observation: "What, then, is a race? It is a vast family of human beings, generally of common blood and language, always of common history, traditions and impulses, who are both voluntarily and involuntarily striving together for the accomplishment of certain more or less vividly conceived ideals of life . . . "
>
> "physical differences of blood, color and cranial measurements" may play a part in race, but "no mere physical distinctions would really define or explain the deeper differences—the cohesiveness and continuity of these groups. The deeper differences are spiritual, psychical differences—undoubtedly based on the physical, but infinitely transcending them" (1999: 209).

These racial ideas, "physical differences of blood, color and cranial measurements," mediated by the bourgeois ideology of nationalism, Wilson further suggests, influenced Du Bois's "double consciousness" construct as the constitutive identity of black people, for in that same essay Du Bois contends:

> . . . . No Negro who has given earnest thought to the situation of his people in America has failed, at some time in life, to find himself at these cross-roads; has failed to ask himself at some time: what, after all, am I? Am I an American or am I a Negro? Can I be both? Or is it my duty to cease to be a Negro as soon as possible and be an American? If I strive as a Negro, am I not perpetuating the very cleft that threatens and separates black and white America? Is not my only possible practical aim the subduction of all that is Negro in me to the American? Does my black blood place upon me any more obligation to assert my nationality than German, or Irish, or Italian blood would (Du Bois, 1971 [1897]: 182)?

This "puzzling dilemma," brought about due to the "physical differences" of the black American as a result of race, i.e., "black blood," which grounds the "deeper differences" of their African psyche and spirituality as demonstrated in "Negro spirituals," as well as the higher ideals they shared with their former white masters, (i.e., being an American), is the basis for black "double consciousness" as the constitutive identity of the black nation. Du Bois demonstrates the construct as social reality in his autobiographical narrative *The Souls of Black Folk*. The scientific contradictions in Du Bois's "The Conservation of Races," however, have led some theorists to refute the idea that Du Bois's "double consciousness" construct avoids the pitfalls of 19th century racial science and ideology to offer a sociohistorical understanding of black identity or consciousness. Anthony Appiah, for example, argues,

> on the face of it, Du Bois' argument in 'The Conservation of Races' is that 'race' is not a scientific—that is, biological—concept. It is a sociohistorical concept. Sociohistorical races each have a 'message' for humanity—a message which derives, in some way, from God's purpose in creating races. The Negro race has still to deliver its full message, and so it is the duty of Negroes to work together—through race organizations—so that this message can be delivered (1985: 25).

But there is tension in Du Bois's alleged sociohistorical conception; "the tension," Appiah continues, "is plain enough in his references to 'common blood'; for this, dressed up with fancy craniometry, a dose of melanin, and some measure for hair curl, is what the scientific notion amounts to. If he has fully transcended the scientific notion, what is the role of this talk about 'blood'?" (1985: 25).

Thus for Appiah, Du Bois's use of "blood" is evidence that his understanding of the realities, "message," of the Negro race is grounded in the context of 19th century racial science and ideology, and therefore a failed sociohistorical attempt at understanding the "souls" or "message" of black folk.

Lucius Outlaw (1996) and Bernard Boxill (1996) disagree with this strict reading of Du Bois's usage of "blood" to explain sociohistorical realities. For Outlaw, "Du Bois has not offered a definition that is intended as 'purely socio-historical.' Rather . . . he seeks to articulate a concept of race that includes both socio-historical or cultural factors (language, history, traditions, 'impulses,' ideals of life) and biological factors . . ." (Outlaw, 1996: 23). Similarly, Boxill, more philosophical than Outlaw, concludes that:

> although Du Bois allowed that cultural and historical differences tend to coincide with differences of 'blood,' he succeeded in providing a conception of race that was historical and cultural, and that he was not committed to the view that

biological differences between human beings determine differences in either their histories or their cultures. Further, although his law of progress stated that the unity required for progress must be based on similarities that are given rather than merely willed, it does not make the racist claim that these similarities are similarities of 'blood,' and that people of the same color must unite simply because they are of the same color (Boxill, 1996: 65).

So, whereas Appiah sees Du Bois's usage of "blood" as his commitment to the racial science and ideology of the 19th century, Outlaw and Boxill view it as an attempt to "use the [19th century] language of race as a political project" (Bell et al, 1996:3). "A political project," according to Robert Gooding-Williams in agreement with Appiah, Du Bois inadequately carries out given his "tacit dependence on a scientific definition of 'race'" (Gooding-Williams, 1996). This dependency turns Du Bois's sociohistorical understanding of the "souls" (consciousness) of black folks into a functionalization of 19th century racial ideology or discourse as mediated by the concept of nation in order to articulate "black" national identity or consciousness in the midst of "white" consciousness (Du Bois, 1984 [1940]; Meier, 1963; Crouch, 1993; Reed, 1997; DeMarco, 1983), what Kirt H. Wilson sees as Du Bois's critical attempt toward a discursive theory of racial identity, "from a study of what race is to a study of what race means" (Wilson, 1999: 209) for black folk.

This functionalization of black racial identity or consciousness in order to define it vis-à-vis "white American consciousness" is reflected in " Of Our Spiritual Strivings" of *The Souls of Black Folk*, which provides us with the often-quoted, racialized bicultural definition of black double-consciousness that has dominated how some social scientists and scholars have come to understand black self-identity in the midst of contemporary social structural arguments, which reiterate nineteenth-century conclusions of black life in America:

After the Egyptian and Indian, the Greek and Roman, the Teuton and Mongolian, the Negro is a sort of seventh son, born with a veil, and gifted with second-sight in this American world,—a world which yields him no true self-consciousness, but only lets him see himself through the revelation of the other world. It is a peculiar sensation, this double-consciousness, this sense of always looking at one's self through the eyes of others, of measuring one's soul by the tape of a world that looks on in amused contempt and pity. One ever feels his twoness,—an American, a Negro; two souls, two thoughts, two unreconciled strivings; two warring ideals in one dark body, whose dogged strength alone keeps it from being torn asunder.

The history of the American Negro is the history of this strife,—this longing to attain self conscious manhood, to merge his double self into a better and truer self. In this merging he wishes neither of the older selves to be lost. He would not Africanize America, for America has too much to teach the world and Africa. He would not bleach his Negro soul in a flood of white Americanism, for he knows that Negro blood has a message for the world. He simply wishes to make it possible for a man to be both a Negro and an American, without being cursed and spit upon by his fellows, without having the doors of opportunity closed roughly in his face (Du Bois, 1995 [1903]: 43-47).

Deconstructed from its reliance on nineteenth-century racial science, this "double-consciousness" or bicultural response to refuting the inferior characterization of black consciousness and define it vis-à-vis "white American consciousness" is more a reflection of Du Bois's ambivalence about American society, rather than an accurate representation of black American culture. In fact, I want to argue here that the construct and its contemporary usage is due in part more to the continual struggles of a particular class of black Americans amidst the contradictory practices of a racist and capitalist modernity, "class racism," which they in turn recursively organize and reproduce as liberal black bourgeois Protestantism, than to a theoretically grounded framework that characterizes the dual "practical consciousness" of the entire "African American community" comprised of liberals, conservatives, Marxists, homosexuals, feminists, Muslims, etc.

THE SOCIOHISTORICAL TURN

The shift, in the mid-to-late twentieth-century, from biological "races" to sociohistorical processes (culture, social structure, or the social relations of production) as the underlying factor in consciousness formation did not rule out the inferiority issues associated with constructions of "blackness," which led to Du Bois's attempt in *The Souls of Black Folk* (1903) at articulating the dual and enduring racial nature of black consciousness. On the contrary, the sociohistorical turn raised some of these same issues as "many racist, liberal and Marxists social scientists argued that blacks had no real culture, that slavery destroyed it, and that what passed as black culture was simply a pathological reaction to whites, a duplication of them or an expression of lower-class culture rather than a specific black culture" (Karenga, 1993: 276). In other words, there is no "Negro-ness," "African-ness," or "blackness," associated with black American life, for these aspects of black life were destroyed during the slavery era (Frazier, 1939; 1957).

Like Du Bois, who in *The Souls of Black Folk* argued for the preservation of black Folk's dual racial nature (African and American), many social theorists then as now responded to these "racist" ideas by pointing to the survival of African culture as evidence that blacks did not completely internalize the negative images of slavery. Thus, black culture or consciousness was viewed as a synthesis of these African survivals (Africanisms) with European cultural norms, giving blacks a "double consciousness" or making them "hybrids" or "bicultural" (Allen, 2001; Asante, 1988, 1990; Billingsley, 1968, 1970, 1993; Blassingame, 1972; Early, 1993; Gilroy, 1993; Gutman, 1976; Herskovits, 1958 [1941]; Holloway, 1990a; Karenga, 1993; Levine, 1977; Lewis, 1993; Lincoln and Mamiya, 1990; Nobles, 1987; Staples, 1978; Stack, 1974; West and Gates, 1997; West, 1993).

These two contentious and controversial contemporary approaches for understanding the nature of black life or ways of being-in-the-world, i.e., consciousness, Maulana Karenga calls, "the pathological-pathogenic and the adaptive-vitality approaches" (1993: 280).

The pathological-pathogenic approach laid out most articulately by E. Franklin Frazier, Gunnar Myrdal, Stanley Elkins, and later Nathan Glazer and Daniel Patrick Moynihan, is predicated on the assumption that the black person is "an exaggerated American" and essentially a "pathological" reaction to whites (Elkins, 1959; Frazier, 1939,1957; Genovese, 1974; Murray, 1984; Moynihan, 1965; Myrdal, 1944; Wilson, 1978, 1987; Sowell, 1975, 1981; Stampp, 1956, 1971). Hence, "[i]n practically all its divergences, American Negro culture is not something independent of general American culture. It is a distorted development, or pathological condition, of the general American culture" (Myrdal, 1944: 928). That is, the black person "is only an American and nothing else. He has no values and culture to guard and protect" (Glazer and Moynihan, 1963: 53). Therefore, the perpetuation of families, in the black community, marked by and conducive to matriarchy, broken and ineffective males, delinquency, economic dependency, poor academic performance, and unwed motherhood are nothing more than pathologies which stem from their reaction to the brutal institutional arrangements of slavery, industrialization, and urbanization, "forces," driven by the capitalist social relations of production of the American social structure, which caused the slaves and their descendants, as E. Franklin Frazier suggests, to "take over, however, imperfectly, the folkways of the American [social] environment, discovering within the patterns of the white man's culture a purpose in life" (Gutman, 1976: 260).

The problem with this social structural approach, like Du Bois's biological determinism, is that it too is deterministic, replacing "race" and "nation" as determinants of consciousness with culture, social structure, or the capitalist social relations of production. That is, black Americans are presented as passive and "impulsive" automatons or "blank slates" programmed by their white masters with a defective (pathological) version of the structural ideology of American society (Frazier, 1966 [1939]: 32). Thus the American capitalist social structure, as recursively organized and reproduced by bourgeois whites, dominates and effaces, by threatening blacks' ontological security, anything "subjectively" African about the black American.

Du Bois in his Hegelian or dialectical parallel to the pathological-pathogenic approach—"[i]t is a peculiar sensation, this double-consciousness, this sense of always looking at one's self through the eyes of others, of measuring one's soul by the tape of a world that looks on in amused contempt and pity"—was able to maintain the distinctiveness and agency of the African, with his reliance on nineteenth-century understanding of race, i.e., biological races each have a message for the world (Du Bois, 1995 [1903]; 1972 [1897]). The structural-functional and Marxist approaches of the pathological-pathogenic school, in contrast, posits that the "other world," the American capitalist world, forced blacks to internalize its negative stereotypes (soulless, poor, immoral, uncultured, irrational, barbaric, affective and emotional) of their material conditions and "blackness," which led to black self-hatred and their attempts to live like bourgeois whites amidst their poor material conditions created by their relations to the means of production (Woodson, 1969; Frazier, 1957; Hare, 1991; Kardiner and Ovesey, 1962).

Alternatively, the adaptive-vitality approach, supplanting Du Bois's concepts of race and nation with culture, contends "that blacks could not possibly live and develop for over three hundred years simply by reacting [to and adopting 'the white man's culture']. On the contrary, blacks [, as a racial class 'for-itself,'] have made self-conscious and self constructive efforts which have contributed to American culture, not simply borrowed from it" (Karenga, 1993: 277). In this understanding, the pathologies or "divergences" of the pathological-pathogenic school are seen as African adaptive responses to the American condition, or "institutional cultural transformations" from Africa to America, which makes the culture of the descendants of slaves "neither African nor American but genuinely Afro-American," a group "identity-in-differential" to that of the American one, which cannot be compared to it (Asante, 1988, 1990; Blassingame, 1972; Gutman, 1976; Herskovits, 1958 [1941]; Levine, 1977; Sudarkasa, 1981). That is, "just as surely as black American family patterns are in part an outgrowth of the descent into slavery, so too are they partly a reflection of the archetypical African institutions and values [, i.e., affective rather than economic approach to family life, collectivity, rather than the individualism which is endemic to European culture, an egalitarian quality to relationships, an extended kin base, etc.,] that informed and influenced the behavior of the Africans who were enslaved in America" (Karenga, 1993: 282-283).

This "adaptive-vitality" response is problematic for two reasons, however. The first is related to the critique mentioned above concerning the structural determinism of the pathological-pathogenic school. That is, there is ambiguity in the concept of a *unified* African cultural inheritance, which for the most part is a biologically determined notion of blackness, structurally organizing the African's way of life against the external structural ideology of white American society.[2] Such a concept, presupposes, however, like Du Bois, a biologically, as opposed to a culturally or structurally, determined uniformity and uniqueness of African cultures institutionalized and practiced within the American social structure, which ethnography and historical records do not completely support (Smith, 1957: 36; Holloway, 1990: 1).[3]

For example, the "adaptive-vitality" school commonly interprets the divergences of the pathological-pathogenic school to be matriarchy, "an improvisational communal consciousness," emotionalism, musical style, and intuition, elements of African culture or racial identity, which blacks have adapted to their American conditions (Gilroy, 1993; Herskovits, 1958 [1941]; Levine, 1977; Sudarkasa, 1981). The problem with this position, however, is that there are numerous cultures (Mali, Berbers, etc.) of Africa among whom these elements are not found. Moreover, there are many other peoples, including whites, among whom these practices have been reported.

This fact leads us to the second problem of the "adaptive-vitality" school, which ties it to the "pathological-pathogenic" school: assessing the impact that the structural ideology of American society, which created "blackness" as a social category for identity construction, but prevented blacks from recursively organizing or reproducing the structural or cultural terms (norms, values, proscriptions and prescriptions) associated with their heterogeneous "Africanness" or "blackness," has had on black Americans and the development of their consciousness. For by assuming the divergences of black American consciousness to be a result of their innate sense of blackness which was to some degree shielded from the institutional arrangements of slavery, the adaptive-vitality school in part overshadows and mystifies the sociocultural impact slavery had on the development of black consciousness, which in their theorizing is, "black consciousness," an element of being that is solely contingent, irrespective of the social environment, on racial (read as cultural) type. Just the same, by assuming the divergences in black consciousness to be nothing more than pathological reactions to American capitalist institutional arrangements, the pathological-pathogenic school denies the agency of black social actors.

These problems point to a serious dilemma of theorizing consciousness or identity formation; that is, how does one demonstrate agency in identity or consciousness formation without overstating the case, diluting criticism of the system or social structure for a sort of biological determinism, as in the case of the adaptive-vitality school? Likewise, the parallel dilemma is how does one emphasize the system or social structure, without contributing to the subjugation of the social actor, as in the case of the pathological-pathogenic school?

THEORY AND METHOD

There is one contemporary social science school, which attempts to address this question of agency and consciousness within the conception of modern society as system or social structure. This is the structurationist or praxis school, commonly associated with Jürgen Habermas (1987 [1981], 1984 [1981]), Pierre Bourdieu (1990 [1980], 1984), and Anthony Giddens (1984) in sociology, and Marshall Sahlins (1976, 1995 [1981]) in anthropology (Crothers, 2003; Ortner, 1984). Elaborated in a series of theoretical works and empirical studies, structurationists or praxis theorists account for agency and consciousness in social structure or system, "by clamping action and structure together in a notion of 'practice' or 'practises'" (Crothers, 2003: 3). That is, structures are not only external to social actors, as in the classic structural functional view, but are also internal rules and resources produced and reproduced by actors "unconsciously" (intuitively) in their practices. From this perspective, accordingly, structure or, sociological speaking, social structure, "may set [(ideological)] conditions to the historical process, but it is dissolved and reformulated in material practice, so that history becomes the realization, in the form of society, of the actual [(embodied rules)] resources people put into play" (Sahlins, 1995 [1981]: 7): consciousness, as a result, refers to "practical consciousness" or the dissolution and reformulation of a social structure's terms (norms, values, prescriptions, and proscriptions) in material practice.

Although this dialectical "clamping together" of structure, praxis, and consciousness descriptively accounts for "the individual moment of phenomenology" by explaining the unanimity, closure, and "intentionality" of a form of human action or sociation, in terms of the capitalist social (material) relations of production, which constitutes the integrative actions of modern society, it fails, however, to account for fully visible alternative forms of practices, i.e., "the variability of the individual *moments* of phenomenology," within the dominant order. Structurationists, like the classic structural functional and structural-Marxist theorizing of the pathological-pathogenic school, fail to see that society and its dominant institutionalized identity is not "one-dimensional" and differentiated by the dialectic (structural contradictions) of capitalist social relations, but is constituted, through power relations, as transition, relation, and difference.

This difference, akin to Jacques Derrida's *différance*, is not biologically (racially) hardwired in the social actor, as the adaptive-vitality school implies, but is a result of self-reflective and non-impulsive social actors, upon internalizing the relative structural terms of their society via linguistic communication, conceiving of and exercising other forms of being-in-the-world from that of the dominant symbolic order and its structural differentiation or relational form (Habermas, 1987 [1981], 1984 [1981]; Giddens, 1984).

By "clamping" action, structure, and consciousness together, i.e., dynamic part/whole totality, however, structurationists, with the exception of Jürgen Habermas's "communicative action" model, do not account for, nor demonstrate, the nature or relation of this non-biologically and non-impulsive determined difference (*différance*) to that of the dominant practices of the social structure. Instead, they re-introduce the problem in a new form: How do we know or *exercise* anything at odds with an embodied received view grounded in and differentiated by structural contradictions, or in contemporary times the social relations of production?

Habermas, through his dual notion of "systems and lifeworld" attempts to resolve this problem of agency within contemporary modern capitalist structures of signification. However, in viewing the system of the political economy as the result of mutually agreed upon rational rules of conduct amongst the various "interpretive communities" of the lifeworld, his theoretical communicative "consensus" model or "organic solidarity" conceives and validates the constituting social conflict that exists between these communities, individual social actors, and those who govern the political economy, as a "crisis" and not as the nature of systems integration within a particular historical social formation. In order to account for the reflexivity of social actors, in other words, Habermas builds on liberalism's distinction between private sphere (lifeworld) and public sphere (system). He places great emphasis on the private sphere or lifeworld as the site for the constitution of indeterminate individual opinions, cultural practices, meanings, etc., and the system or public sphere as the site for and constituted by the mutually agreed upon rational rules of conduct which are sanctioned for societal or social cohesion (Habermas, 1989). In emphasizing this individual, social whole relationship, however, he largely neglects the ideological (class, sex, gender, race) basis by which the "system" or contemporary "public sphere," the social "whole," was itself constituted against the identity and interest of "other" groups or publics, women, people of color, homosexuals, etc. (Fraser, 1996).

Be that as it may, it is in building on and against Habermas's conflict-less and normatively utopic liberal bourgeois model of society and its relation to the individual I propose to account for this question of black practical consciousness, which eludes the structural-functionalism and structural-Marxism of the pathological-pathogenic approach and is overshadowed (but at the same time also reintroduced through a form of genetic determinism) by the biological take of the adaptive-vitality position.[4]

While I accept the structurationist understanding that structural practice and consciousness are indeed "dual," modern society or social structure is a "mechanicistic," as opposed to Jürgen Habermas's "organic," relation of domination. The modern social world is constituted and integrated through the dialectical interaction between a dominating "practical consciousness," embodied and recursively organized and reproduced by a majority of social actors, who "change or maintain a potentially malleable social life-world" (Archer, 1985: 60) against fully visible marginalized non-biologically (non-racially) determined "alternative" practices (*différance*). These "alternative practices," "counterpublics," or categorical boundaries relationally delimit, and thereby help constitute, the dominant social world or society as marginalized ego-centered identities-in-differential existing "for-themselves" as opposed to ones "in-themselves" suggestive of or reproduced by structural differentiation or the relational logic (binary rules for inclusion and exclusion) of those in power position in the society or social structure.

This discontinuous conceptualization of structure and action accounts for the "variability of the individual moments of phenomenology." It does so, by giving the social actor choice (through rationality and reflection) in the constitution of his or her practical consciousness (es), which constitute society not as a Habermasian (1987 [1981]) "organic" communicative utopic paradise governed by the "mutually agreed upon" rational rules of the political economy, but as a "mechanicistic" hierarchical and conflictual order: a dominating recursively reproduced action (structuring consciousness) differentially related to marginalized and discriminated against "identities-in differential," or other "forms of sociation," i.e., social movements, "existing for themselves," which relationally delimits, and thereby helps constitute, the dominant form of societal interaction that is the public sphere.

DISCUSSION AND CONCLUSION

Using this variant of structuration theory, I undertake an "ideal type" analysis of the sociohistorical origins and nature of black consciousness by applying this theoretical frame to the most significant aspect of black life within the American Protestant capitalist bourgeois social structure (Weber, 1958 [1904-1905]), which has shaped black "practical consciousness": the institution of slavery, the organization of work, which structured black social relations within the American "racial capitalist" social structure, and the response of blacks to its legacy, racial prejudice and class discrimination.

Specifically, I reinterpret the historiography of how the institution of slavery impacted and re-shaped African practical consciousnesses. Africans were introduced into the American Protestant capitalist social structure as slaves. Given their economic material conditions, their African practical consciousnesses were represented by American whites as primitive forms of being-in-the-world to that of the dominant American white Protestant bourgeois social order (Patterson, 1982: 38).

From this theoretical perspective, and in keeping with the dominant structural interpretation of the pathological-pathogenic school, I illustrate the structural forces—race, class, and status—that eventually, under the "contradictory principles of marginality and integration" (Patterson, 1982: 46), shaped the *majority* of African consciousness as a "racial class-in-itself" (blacks), a "caste in class," forced to embody the structural terms (bourgeois ideals in the guise of the protestant ethic) of the dominant American (capitalist) social relations of production, over all other "alternative" African adaptive responses to its then organizational form, slavery.

This embodiment of bourgeois ideals, in the guise of the protestant ethic, by the majority of Africans amidst their poor material conditions created by the social relations of Protestant capitalist organization, I conclude, eventually made the struggle to obtain equality of opportunity, distribution, and recognition with their white Protestant bourgeois counterparts amidst racial and class discrimination their goal. To this end, the struggle for freedom was nothing more than a black middle class phenomenon as the more "liberal" arm of the best of the house servants, artisans, and free blacks from the North, acting as a structurally differentiated "racial class-for-itself," sought to define the black situation for all blacks, in terms of the society's Protestant bourgeois ideals (temperance, economic gain for its own sake, and "good moral character"), which they acquired through "ideological apparatuses" defined by their white capitalist masters who viewed black poverty, emotionalism, intuition, disobedience, "immorality," and "barbarity" as contrary to white civilized Protestantism. Thus, as I will further demonstrate through an analysis of W.E.B. Du Bois's *habitus* or "practical consciousness," the embodiment of the Protestant ethic, the agential moments of the American social structure, amidst the racial discrimination faced by blacks as they sought and seek to organize and reproduce this ethic in order to improve their material conditions or obtain economic gain and recognition, is the sole reason for this double consciousness or biculturation that the adaptive-vitality school and Du Bois attempt to externally validate.

Put differently, I conclude, from my structurationist interpretation of the black Americans struggle for freedom to better their material conditions, and Du Bois's particular embodiment of that struggle, that their struggle "for opportunity-enhancing and outcome-based egalitarian statist policies" (Wilson,

2000: 75) was neither driven by the praxis of their African ways of being-in-the-world, nor a "double consciousness" /bicultural (Afro/African-American) way of being-in-the-world embedded in traditions, value-systems, ideas, and institutional forms which oppose the Protestant capitalist social order of the American social structure. Rather, the "black" struggle for freedom to better their material conditions, based on "opportunity-enhancing and outcome-based egalitarian statist policies," was due to the fact that the majority of "blacks," who led the freedom struggle, internalized and embodied the "traditions, value-systems, ideas, and institutional forms" of the American bourgeois social structure, against fully visible, albeit ontologically insecure, "other" black "practical-consciousnesses" (African structural practices, black nationalism or pan-Africanism, conservatism, homosexuality, black communism, the pathology of the black poor, black feminism, etc.),[5] thus measuring or assessing their successes and failures, and reacting to the "other" visible black practical consciousnesses in terms of the American protestant social structure's rules of conduct, which they did and do sanction (Woodson, 1933; Frazier, 1957; Hare, 1965 [1991]; Kardiner and Ovesey, 1962 [1951]; hooks, 1981, 1994).

Accordingly, it follows, it is only in relation to the "class racism" of the liberal black bourgeoisie's "form of consciousness" or practical consciousness that all other black forms of being in the American capitalist social structure become, and are, pathological-pathogenic or adaptive.[6] That is to say, as we will see through a structurationist analysis of W.E.B. Du Bois's (an initial paragon of black middle class interest) *habitus* or practical consciousness, it is in terms of liberal black (male) middle class push for equality of opportunity, distribution, and recognition for all blacks amidst the discriminatory affects of white American society that the "double-consciousness" of black American consciousness must be understood.

Du Bois's double consciousness, which he is so intuitively[7] aware of, is unlike Antonio Gramsci's "two theoretical consciousnesses" (the practical consciousness of the society and a superficially explicit or verbal one, which opposes the former, existing in one body), but more akin to Marx's "ideology."

Gramsci's "two theoretical consciousnesses" imply that the social actor is divided between two hegemonic articulatory principles, one practical and the other ideal with its own articulatory principles.

Du Bois's ideals and practices, which stem from the articulatory principles of one historical bloc, are one and the same. In fact, he uses the concepts (race, nation, class) of the historical bloc to ideologically define the consciousness of the black nation in relation to that of the white power elites, whose contempt for blacks' poor material conditions Du Bois intended to reject by pointing to blacks' historical past in order to uplift them to whites' bourgeois status-position once the doors of opportunity were opened.

Hence, Du Bois in *The Souls* is ideologically using double consciousness to convict the society, because of its discriminatory practices, for not identifying with its liberal Protestant bourgeois values, because they close the door of opportunity in the face of black Americans who are cursed and spat upon for their lowly "poor" racial class position, which he believes can easily be transformed once the doors are open.

To this ideological and practical end for equality of opportunity and recognition, Du Bois's double consciousness is more suggestive, in the words of Frantz Fanon (1967[1952]), of the struggle, the *desire*, of members of the black (male) bourgeoisie, to prove to their former colonizers, "at all costs, the richness of their thought, the equal value of their intellect" (10)—i.e., that they can be just as human (an agent of the protestant ethic and its practice the spirit of capitalism) as the colonizers are—against their *derision* for the ontologically insecure but fully visible (albeit distorted) "other" "pathological-pathogenic" understanding of themselves, as exercised by the black poor (a class in-itself) and nationalist leaning blacks (a class for-itself), their colonizers discriminated against them for.

Hence, this "doubleness," the *ambivalence* which arises in members of the liberal black (male) bourgeoisie when discriminated against as they struggle to prove their self-worth as agents of the Protestant ethic against negative stereotypes, commonly associated with nationalist leaning blacks and lower class blacks, used to prevent them from achieving their aim for economic gain, equality, and recognition is the "two souls, two thoughts, two unreconciled strivings; two warring ideals in one dark body, whose dogged strength alone keeps . . . [them] from being torn asunder" (Du Bois, 1995 [1903]: 45)—as opposed to two distinct cultural epistemes for understanding the world implicit in the reliance on the biological framework—which Du Bois, in *The Souls,* autobiographically intuits as the racialized "double consciousness" of Black folk, and which the adaptive-vitality school attempts to externally validate.[8]

NOTES

1. This is not the case today, as the black underclass is slowly becoming the bearers of ideological and linguistic domination in the larger society.

2. My use of hegemony does not describe the African influence as an attempt to subdue and dominate the American; on the contrary, it is used to highlight the hegemonic intentions of the adaptive-vitality school's interpretation of "black culture" vis-à-vis individual black social actors.

3. This position is made famous by liberals, pan-Africanist, and nationalist leaning blacks who explain the divergences of black life by seeking to "externally validate"

Du Bois's double consciousness construct in a nationalist position of their own, or as a sought of counter movement or culture to modernity (American culture).

4. It is often the criticism levied against Habermas that his model is conflictless and utopic. My position assumes this criticism because inherent in Habermas's model is the assumption that in order for communicative discourse to take place, the discussants must share the underlying rules of discourse that frames their discourse. It is precisely because the African was an "other," which prevented communicative discourse between themselves and Europeans. In that case, domination, and not communicative discourse, determined their social interaction.

5. This conclusion refutes both the adaptive-vitality and pathological-pathogenic schools' positions. The premise here is that "black consciousness" is not a result of an innate sense of blackness, for then all "blacks" would have one singular biologically (i.e., racially) determined consciousness. On the contrary, the practical consciousnesses of black folks are multiple and diverse (as a result of their (blacks) varying responses to American institutional arrangements) differentially related to, and delimited by, the dominating agential moments or responses of those (i.e., the black bourgeoisie) who have led the black struggle for freedom by recursively organizing and reproducing the agential moments of the American capitalist social structure in order to prove their self-worth within, given the society's discriminatory practices, which in that instance comes off as (given their marginalization) the contradictory practices of their society.

6. E. Franklin Frazier and the pathological-pathogenic school assess black family life in terms of the structural variables of the American social structure: the patriarchical, Protestant nuclear family. Even Du Bois (see his work *The Philadelphia Negro* 1899) in his radical understanding of black life, understands their pathological conditions in terms of his protestant structural upbringing. It is a misunderstanding to see this phenomenon as a sign of self-hatred; on the contrary, this represents attempts by agents of the protestant ethic to understand the conditions of black folk in terms of their structural paradigm. This is a practice which, as Stanford M. Lyman and Arthur J. Vidich (1985) point out, dominated early American sociological work and continues to do so as can be seen in the work of the black American sociologist William Julius Wilson.

7. See Robert B. Stepto's (1985 [1979]) "The Quest of the Weary Traveler" W.E.B. Du Bois's *The Souls of Black Folk*," for an understanding of his essay as a "narrative" as opposed to a "social scientific study" (172).

8. Ernest Allen (1992; 2002) makes this same claim. However, his position that Du Bois's use of terms such as "double consciousness," "double ideals," and "twoness" are not in complete accord with the traditional biculturalist interpretations of the assimilationist/nationalist readings, because "the fact remains that in *The Souls of Black Folk* he neglected to use those terms in that explicit way" (1992, 262), is mistaken. For Allen's attempted "fix" and "narrow" interpretations of these terms is done at the expense of the broader context of nineteenth century (hegemonic) social scientific thought, which framed Du Bois's usage of them. That is, Allen's Frazierian (1957: 25) interpretation of Du Boisian double consciousness as the "arrested mentality of the Talented Tenth [(the black educated elites)] . . . deriving from the collapse of imputed 'double ideals' [(the

socialization of the black elites in such a way as to lead them to disparage their social origins and to seek an especial kind of recognition, that is to say respect, from the dominant society—one which generally would be denied)] of this class" (1992, 269-273) fails to encapsulate the fact that the early Du Bois is suggesting that there *is* a distinct "Negroness," derived from "black blood," (i.e., African spirituality inherited in the African by their "black blood"), regardless of the Talented Tenth's achievements, which allows for their self-estrangement. Dickson D. Bruce Jr. (1992) makes this latter point— Du Bois attempts to synthesize the psychology and sociophilosophy of the nineteenth-century with its understanding of race in order to understand "black" identity formation or consciousness in the midst of "white" consciousness—clearly in his essay, "W.E.B. Du Bois and the Idea of Double Consciousness."

Bruce draws on Du Bois's possible familiarity with all the background on double consciousness from literary and medical sources to conclude that Du Bois's use of the idea of double consciousness, to characterize issues of race, emerges out of his conflating of European Romanticism and American Transcendentalism, and the field of psychology while holding on to nineteenth century racial theory (Bruce, 1992: 299-300). In the former, according to Bruce, especially in Emerson's work, the idea of "double-consciousness" refers "to a problem in the life of one seeking to take a Transcendental perspective on self and world .... [t]he double consciousness plaguing the Transcendentalist summarized the downward pull of life in society—including the social forces inhibiting genuine self-realization—and the upward pull of communion with the divine ... " (300). In the case of the latter (psychological sources), the term "was applied to cases of split personality ... "(300). For Bruce,

[a]lthough Du Bois used "double consciousness" to refer to at least three different issues—including first the real power of white stereotypes in black life and thought and second the double consciousness created by the practical racism that excluded every black American from the mainstream of society, the double consciousness of being both an American and not an American—by double consciousness Du Bois referred most importantly to an internal conflict in the African American individual between what was "African" and what was "American." It was in terms of this third sense that the figurative background [(its Transcendental and Romantic grounding)] to "double consciousness" gave the term its most obvious support, because for Du Bois the essence of a distinctive African consciousness was its spirituality, a spirituality based in Africa but revealed among African Americans in their folklore, their history of patient suffering, and their faith. In this sense, double consciousness related particularly to Du Bois's efforts to privilege the spiritual in relation to the materialistic, commercial world of white America (301).

Just the same, Bruce goes on to point out, as telling as the figurative background to double consciousness may have been, that background was supplemented in important ways by the psychological sources, which Du Bois utilized to characterize the Transcendental duality in terms of the psychological emphasis on split personality. In this sense, the spiritual nature (African) and the materialistic commercial world (American) that was the double consciousness of black folk, which like someone diagnosed with split personality, were viewed as two distinctive oppositional personalities (African and American) within a single body (304).

"Such a background of ideas and facts," as Bruce concludes, "made the concept of double consciousness especially useful to Du Bois, given his desire to develop a positive sense of racial distinctiveness out of a distinctively African heritage. Ideas of race and behavior were problematic in the late nineteenth century . . . , [for] 'Race' itself carried biological connotations—connotations not entirely absent from Du Bois's discussions—that were troublesome, since biological notions of race served mainly to ground those beliefs concerning black inferiority which were generally accepted by whites" (305).

What Du Bois attempted to do, was to portray positively, and emphasize the integrity of, blacks' distinctive nature—their African mode of thought, associated with their race, and their internalization of the American—against the inferiority understanding whites posited based simply on the African's racial type. This standpoint did not refute race but was an attempt, "[i]n the absence of any kind of adequate idea of cultural relativism," (305), to portray and articulate the experiences of Black folk, their consciousness, based on what race was as articulated in the nineteenth century (Appiah, 1985).

Chapter Two

A Structural Reading of African American History in America

In order to understand better black American consciousness and Du Bois's double consciousness construct, this chapter explores African American "practical consciousness" as it has developed within Max Weber's "protestant ethic and the spirit of capitalism" cultural characterization of American society (Weber, 1958; Hudson and Coukos, 2005; Cohen, 2002; Jones, 1971). The chapter highlights the dialectical relation, between blacks from Africa and white Protestant agents of the American capitalist social structure that eventually shaped the majority of African American consciousness to a large extent as the embodiment of the purposive-rationality of "the protestant ethic and the spirit of capitalism."

Many scholars of the pathological-pathogenic school conclude that this antagonistic practical interrelationship eventually made the majority of black consciousness, within the American, white, Protestant bourgeois symbolic order, nothing more than a "poor" (pathological-pathogenic) or "absurd" form of American consciousness due to racial and class differentiation (Frazier, 1939, 1957; Stampp, 1956, 1971; Elkins, 1959; Genovese, 1974; Moynihan, 1965; Wilson, 1978, 1996).[1] The adaptive-vitality school, supplanting Du Bois's concepts of race and nation with culture, on the contrary, argues that blacks developed a Du Boisian double-consciousness, their African racial practical consciousness, and the American one characterized not solely by the Protestantism of the American capitalist symbolic order, but also by "an improvisational communal consciousness," emotionalism, musical style, and intuition rooted in a folk culture grounded in their Africanness or, what amounts to the same thing, their sense of blackness (Levine, 1977; Gutman, 1976; Blassingame, 1972; Holloway, 1990; Karenga, 1993; Gilroy, 1993; Allen, 2001).

My structural understanding of the relationship refutes both of these positions. My structural reading supposes that social actors or groups never operate from a transcendental or objective standpoint. Instead, they constitute an historical structure of interpretative understanding, which is thus always already engaged in the activity of interpretation within the *a priori* structures of signification of those who control the resources of the material resource framework within which the historical structure of interpretative understanding is ensconced. In fact, the historical structure of interpretative understanding of those in power position becomes the ideological superstructure for maintaining control of "other" interpretative understandings and the material resource framework.

This does not mean that social actors are unable to transcend the interpretative structures of signification of those in power position. On the contrary, consciousness, and by logical association, agency is contingent on either the integrative rules of conduct, recursively organized and reproduced in material practice, of those who control the resources of the material resource framework, or the reformulation, through the deferment of meaning in ego-centered communicative action, of these rules of conduct in material practices for "other" marginalized forms of being-in-the-world, "identities-in-differential," which are in turn symbolically used by those in power positions to maintain their power position, and relationally delimit their historical structure of interpretative understandings and practices.

Hence, agency or more appropriately, practical consciousness is not inherently dual, defined solely by a structure and its contradictions, which social actors recursively organize and reproduce in the material resource framework; instead, it (social action) is multiple and diverse resulting from the dominant social structure and its contradictions as well as the self-reflexivity of social agents despite structural constraints. In fact, it is the social actors in the power positions of a particular social structure who attempt to make "practical consciousness" dual; they symbolically name, define, and utilize the "other" actions of social actors to maintain control and relationally differentiate and integrate their own practical consciousness or discursive practice as the constitutive identity of the society.

In this theoretical framework, which posits the constitution of society to be the result of two contradictory principles, marginality and integration, human society is seen as a Durkheimian "mechanical solidarity" or social structure constituted by social actors, with a distinct form of Being-in-the-world, (practical) consciousness, who marginalize and discriminate against "other" behaviors or forms of (practical) consciousnesses different from their own in order to integrate the social practices of the society.

It is within this solidarity or constitution of modern American Protestant society, as opposed to the liberal bourgeois "organic" or rational model proposed by Jürgen Habermas's (1987 [1981]) communicative action model, my structural reading attempts to understand African American practical consciousness and Du Bois's double consciousness construct.

The premise that unfolds here is that black American consciousness became, as a result of blacks' social integration into the white, American protestant, bourgeois social structure, as marginalized "non-beings" (Patterson, 1982: 38-42), multiple and diverse.[2] They were differentially related to, and delimited by, the dominating purposive-rationality of the liberal black (male) bourgeoisie. A bourgeoisie which, as a structurally differentiated "racial-class-in-itself" serving as a reference group for other blacks, became the bearers of ideological domination for black folk and led the black struggle for freedom against slavery and marginalization by recursively organizing and reproducing the integrative Protestant "practical consciousness" of the American social structure. This they did in order to obtain equality of opportunity, distribution, and recognition, against the contemptuous gaze of its white agents and the agents of other black adaptive responses to enslavement.

Consequently, from this understanding, the Du Boisian double consciousness the adaptive-vitality school attempts to externally validate can best be understood as the ambivalence that arises within the black bourgeoisie because of the structural differentiation, produced among blacks by the economic and racial stratification ("class racism"), of the American symbolic order, as opposed to a distinct ethos from that of the American protestant bourgeois middle class type which defines the black community as a distinct nation constituted by its biculturalism.

Unlike the position of the pathological-pathogenic school, it is not my view that this phenomenon, the *adaptive* response of many blacks to recursively organize and reproduce the purposive rationality of the American social structure defined by the accumulation of capital to prove one's predestination in a "calling," against their original African practical consciousness, was a result of self-hatred or a lack of black agency under the patriarchal brutality and oppressiveness of "racial" slavery.[3]

Quite the reverse, this was a self-directed phenomenon driven by the more liberal segment of the enslaved and discriminated against black population, the "best" of the house servants, mulattoes, artisans, and the educated free Negro from the North, who sought (by positioning themselves as a reference group for the black community), as a "racial" "class-for-itself," to define the black situation for all blacks of the American social structure along its Protestant and capitalist ethos, which they took to be the nature of reality and existence as such.

Given this response amongst the more free and powerful majority of the descendants of African slaves, who were barred from organizing and reproducing their African institutions within the material resource framework of the American Protestant social and economic order, it is in terms of the structural variables (i.e., class and status, given the economic basis for the social relations of the society) of the society, not other factors, that black consciousness in America can be and has been assessed and determined. For all other forms of practical-consciousness amongst blacks within American society were defined and relationally delimited as "other" by these blacks, the "best" of the house servants, mulattoes, artisans, and the educated free Negro from the North, who, when they became institutional regulators within the American social structure, delimited or represented the "proper" and "pure" way of being-in-the-world for all blacks in terms of Protestant bourgeois practical consciousness, i.e., interest, ideals, habitus, etc.

Thus, "after the end of the [(slave)] trade in America in the latter half of the eighteenth and early part of the nineteenth centuries [Africanisms] importance as an explanation of slave personality declines: only about 400,000 native-born Africans had been brought to the United States before 1807 [(the slave trade, as sanctioned by the US Constitution, legally ended in 1808)]. Since an overwhelming percentage of nineteenth-century Southern slaves were native Americans" (Blassingame, 1972: 39), they, about 3,953,760 of the black population at the outbreak of the Civil War, had to construct their identity or consciousness as a deployable unit of the American social structure in relation to and led by "the best of the house servants, who were freed by their masters, [and] the educated free Negro from the North," who together numbered about 500,000, twelve percent of the total black population, "at the outbreak of the Civil War"[4] (See Table 2.1).

So, as my reinterpretation of the black or African experience within the American protestant symbolic order will demonstrate, it is not that black Americans have a "double consciousness" or are bicultural. The majority, according to my theoretical reading of the historical experiences of blacks, adopted a singular practical consciousness, the Protestant ethic of the society, which structured the developing slave community and culture, which they incorporate, or incorporated them, by warring (i.e., discriminating) against other (feminists, nationalists, Catholics, Muslims, etc.) fully visible alternative forms of being-in-the-world available to a minority of blacks and some whites, who became marginalized and discriminated against, within the social structure, by whites and the black bourgeoisie, who are only distinguishable from one another by skin color.[5]

Subsequently, my argument as it unfolds is that it is this ambivalence, desire and derision, as opposed to a black dualistic orientation, that is Du Bois's double consciousness: the *desire* of members of the liberal black bourgeoisie and their descendants, the "new middle class," to prove to their former colonizers, "at all costs, the richness of their thought, the equal value of their in-

Table 2.1. Growth of the Slave and Free Negro Population in the United States 1790-1860

	NEGRO POPULATION			
		Free		
CENSUS YEAR	Total	Number	Per Cent	Slave
1860	4,441,830	488,070	11.0	3,953,760
1850	3,638,808	134,495	11.9	3,204,313
1840	2,873,648	386,293	13.4	2,487,355
1830	2,328,642	319,599	13.7	2,009,043
1820	1,771,656	233,634	13.2	1,538,022
1810	1,377,808	186,446	13.5	1,191,362
1800	1,002,037	108,435	10.8	893,602
1790	757,181	59,557	7.9	697,624

Note. Adapted From *The American Negro: His History and Literature* (p. 5), by E. Franklin Frazier, 1968, New York: Arno Press and The New York Times. Copyright 1968 by Arno Press, Inc.

tellect" (Fanon, 10)—i.e., that they can be just as human (an agent of the protestant ethic and its practice, the spirit of capitalism) as they are—against their *derision* for the discriminatory practices of their white counterparts who used and use the ontologically insecure but fully visible "other" understanding of themselves as exercised by the black poor and nationalist leaning blacks to name, define, and bar them from achieving economic gain, equality, and recognition in the American Protestant bourgeois social order.

Hence Du Bois's construct was more metaphorical and ideological rather than literally highlighting the duality of the black nation.

THE HISTORICAL CONSTITUTION OF AMERICAN SOCIETY OR MODERNITY

In order to understand the bourgeois ideological basis of Du Bois's double consciousness, it is necessary to reconstruct the constitution of the society within which black American consciousness was and is continually being constituted. The Protestant ethic, as Max Weber (1958) points out, represents what was understood, the set of values—rationality, hard work, economic gain as a sign of one's predestination, systematic use of time, and a strict asceticism with respect to worldly pleasures and goods—which he claims gave rise to the contemporary capitalist practices that constitute modern societies, and thus American capitalist society, and the existing configuration of bureaucratic power relations within which black practical consciousness developed.

The purposive-rationality of these Protestant ideas and practices, mediated and overdetermined by the concepts of race and nation, in other words, historicized social positions, based on racial and national identity and economic gain for its own sake through the accumulation of capital or profit in a "calling," by which social actors or subjects were differentiated and subjugated (predestined or capitalists/damned or laborers) in the society.

This framework differs from both Marxist and non-Marxist structural interpretations of the constitution of modern society in that it begins with the cultural (ideal) conceptions that structured the social integrative practices that gave rise to the society, while the Marxist and neo-Marxist schools derive the terms from which they begin their analysis from the (material) social relations of production. These two viewpoints, systems and social integration, as my structural approach implies, are inextricably linked, however. In other words, although we are able to think these two approaches apart as idealism and materialism, they are not necessarily entirely separable in reality.

Weber defines a capitalistic economic action

> as one which rests on the expectation of profit by the utilization of opportunities for exchange, that is on (formally) peaceful chances of profit. Acquisition by force (formally and actually) follows its own particular laws, and it is not expedient, however little one can forbid this, to place it in the same category with action which is, in the last analysis, oriented to profits from exchange. Where capitalist acquisition is rationally pursued, the corresponding action is adjusted to calculations in terms of capital. This means that the action is adapted to a systematic utilization of goods or personal services as means of acquisition in such a way that, at the close of a business period, the balance of the enterprise in money assets (or, in the case of a continuous enterprise, the periodically estimated money value of assets) exceeds the capital, i.e. [,] the estimated value of the material means of production used for acquisition in exchange (Weber, 1958: 17-18).

Although this relationship appears paradoxical, since protestant beliefs did not embrace the idea of economic gain for its own sake,

> Weber's argument is that the rational pursuit of the ultimate values of the ascetic Protestantism characteristic of sixteenth-and seventeenth-century Europe led people to engage in disciplined work; and that disciplined and rational organization of work as a duty is the characteristic feature of modern capitalism—its unique ethos or spirit (Marshall, 1998: 534).

Thus,

> The crucial link to Protestantism comes through the latter's notion of the calling of the faithful to fulfil their duty to God in the methodical conduct of their

everyday lives. This theme is common to the beliefs of the Calvinist and neo-Calvinist churches of the Reformation. Predestination is also an important belief, but since humans cannot know who is saved (elect) and who is damned, this creates a deep inner loneliness in the believer. In order therefore to create assurance of salvation, which is itself a sure sign (or proof) of election, diligence in one's calling (hard work, systematic use of time, and a strict asceticism with respect to worldly pleasures and goods) is highly recommended—so-called 'this-worldly asceticism'. In general terms, however, the most important contribution of Protestantism to capitalism was the spirit of rationalization that it encouraged. The relationship between the two is deemed by Weber to be one of elective affinity (Marshall, 1998: 535).

This affinity, between the Protestantism of a sect and purposive-rationality, gave rise to the *economic* organization of modern society (Polanyi, 2001), as the ideals (rationally calculating individuals attempting to prove their predestination, which was reflected in their economic gains) of a form of Protestantism were rationally incorporated into the world through the bureaucratic organization of the material resource framework around the state and economy. That is, bureaucratic means or structural practices (purposive-formal-rational action to organize the lived world) were established, or already existing material elements were re-conceptualized by a sect of rich, white, Protestant, men.

These men were a discriminated against "other" minority in the Feudal social structure of Europe of the middle ages, who left Europe and reformulated society, in the form of the American social structure, by recursively organizing and reproducing their "other" form of being-in-the-world, i.e., Protestantism and the spirit of capitalism. This they did in the rules of conduct of the new American society formulated to facilitate the relational logic, ends (substantive rationality), of their form of Protestantism: economic gain, or loss, as a sign of one's election or "damned-ness" in a particular "calling," which "embedded" social or cultural relations in what became the modern American political-economic system.

The endless accumulation of economic gain, capital, or profit became "the defining characteristic and *raison d' être* of this [social] system," which over time pushed "towards the commodification of everything, the absolute increase of world production, and a complex and sophisticated social division of labor based on class" or the amount of capital (economic gain) one had accumulated (Balibar and Wallerstein, 1991: 107). As Jürgen Habermas concludes of this process by which the substantive-rationality of a form of Protestantism, "the spirit of capitalism," came to dominate modern times by the purposive-rational action of its power agents:

> ... economic production is organized in a capitalist manner, with rationally calculating entrepreneurs [(the predestined prosper)]; public administration is

organized in a bureaucratic manner, with juristically trained, specialized officials—that is, they are organized in the form of private enterprises and public bureaucracies. The relevant means for carrying out their tasks are concentrated in the hands of owners and leaders; membership in these organizations is made independent of ascriptive properties [(today, maybe, but not the case for this type of society's early formation)]. By these means, organizations gain a high degree of internal flexibility and external autonomy. In virtue of their efficiency, the organizational forms of the capitalist economy and the modern state administration establish themselves in other action systems to such an extent that modern societies fit the picture of "a society of organizations," even from the standpoint of lay members (Habermas, 1987 [1981]: 306).

In this understanding of the origins and organizational basis of modernity, and its paragon, modern American capitalist society, where "the cultural struggle for distinction is intricately connected to the economic distribution of material goods, which it both legitimates and reproduces" (Gartman, 2002: 257), Weber's explanation, as Jürgen Habermas points out,

> . . . refers in the first instance not to the establishment of the labor markets that turned abstract labor power into an expense in business calculations, but to the "spirit of capitalism," that is, to the mentality characteristic of the purposive-rational economic action of the early capitalist entrepreneurs. Whereas Marx took the mode of production to be the phenomenon in need of explanation, and investigated capital accumulation as the new mechanism of system integration, Weber's view of the problem turns the investigation in another direction. For him the explanans is the conversion of the economy and state administration over to purposive-rational action orientations; the changes fall in the domain of forms of social integration. At the same time, this new form of social integration made it possible to institutionalize the money mechanism, and thereby new mechanisms of system integration (Habermas, 1987 [1981]: 313).

These two analytic levels are not separate if the understanding of the constitution of modernity is understood through my structural and organizational logic. The argument from this position is that the "predestined," white Protestant entrepreneurial males, a once marginalized group in pre-modern or feudal Europe, by re-conceptualizing and maintaining the control of the then feudal market and state, reified their Protestant "practical consciousness." This cultural value they rationalized with reality and existence as such, in institutions, the capitalist market economy and bourgeois state, operating "through materialized metaphors beyond logical or empirical proof, on ungroundable premises, on nonobservable substances" (Friedland, 2002: 384), in order to mechanically and systemically direct the agential moments or purposive-rationality of all social actors for the sole purpose of accumulating economic gain (Marx's "capital accumulation") as a sign of one's election or progress.[6]

To this end (the organization of work for economic gain or profit) modern society was mechanically constituted as white Protestant males, i.e., believing themselves to be "predestined," came, as a social class, not without contradictions, to militarily dominate and control the ontological security of the world and its people, who they interpellated as the damned or laborers working in order to (re) produce economic gain for those (predestined) who owned the means and modes of work or production. To put the matter simply, the logic here is that "the spirit of capitalism," which is characteristic of modernity in general and American society in particular, is the discursive practice or purposive rationality of a form of cultural Protestantism that gave rise to the class identity of social actors, who became differentiated by their relation to the means and mode of work in modern societies.

It should also be mentioned that modern society itself became a dialectical totality that underwent reproduction and transformation based on the internal contradictions, i.e., class differentiation, based upon capital accumulation, motivated by the desire to acquire capital or economic gain for its own sake (Balibar and Wallerstein, 1991; Smith, 1996).

Be that as it may, it is not the position here, however, that the "class racism" (Étienne Balibar's term) that would come to characterize the "white" American protestant bourgeois order is to be deduced from capitalist relations of production. As Etienne Balibar observes, "[mo]netary circulation and the exploitation of wage labour do not logically entail a single determinate form of state. Moreover, the realization space which is implied by accumulation — the world capitalist market — has within it an intrinsic tendency to transcend any [racial and] national limitations that might be instituted by determinate fractions of social capital or imposed by 'extra-economic' means" (Balibar, 1991: 89). Instead, the racial/national formation of the American state, it seems, has its development in the structure of its own concrete historical development and form as opposed to a "bourgeois project," which is a historical myth "taken over by Marxism from liberal philosophies of history" (Balibar, 1991: 89).

We might overcome this liberal view through my structural perspective, which sees the constitution of society through the power relations highlighted by Weber within a specific historical social formation (the American nation state), which would, after nationalizing and ethnicizing its population to resolve an internal contradiction in their Protestant ethic (slavery in the face of Christian brotherhood or human equality), come to constitute and direct the world capitalist market in order to accumulate profits or economic gain by modifying other social formations through the prism of its own local social formation, the racialization and nationalization of the protestant ethic and the spirit of capitalism.[7]

THE HISTORICAL CONSTITUTION OF AFRICANNESS IN THE AMERICAN RACIAL-CAPITALIST SOCIAL FORMATION

The distinct constitution of the American racial-capitalist social formation within a capitalist world economy highlights the purposive-rational action of rich, white, Protestant men. This becomes obscured if the focus is solely on the determinism of the division of labor in the logic of capital accumulation as posited by most Marxists, or the notion of "primitive accumulation" posited by classic liberal thinkers. In both cases, the class basis of the arguments fail to account for and underplays the status roles of race, gender, sexuality, etc. in the constitution of the American racial gendered capitalist social formation.

Just the same, the "communicative action" contemporary liberal discourse of Jürgen Habermas which posits the political economy of the state as the product of the "communicative action" amongst the various status and party groups of the "public sphere" also obscures the purposive-rational action of rich, white, Protestant men, which in turn distorts the agential initiative of blacks in the society.

Habermas's "communicative action" postulates the variability of social practices only in theory, and in a normatively "utopic" communicative paradise that distorts the social conflict that arises between groups whose different province of meaning and action differs from those who absorb the purposive-rationality of the social structure as communicative discourse. He underplays, in other words, the power relations (marginalization or segregation) by which the protestant agents of "the spirit of capitalism" constituted the "public sphere" of their solidarity as a cultural system (Fraser, 1997).

This, as in the formation of the American nation state or social system was not simply done "organically" through communicative purposive rational action amongst the power agents of the society, but "mechanically" as Weber's "iron cage" thesis implies.[8] That is, it is not the case that white protestant male social actors constituted modernity, in general, or American society in particular, as a systemic framework or totality arrived at through mutually agreed upon rational rules of conduct which were sanctioned. To the contrary, the discourse of modernity and American society resulted from their (rich, white, protestant men) substantive cultural values and practices, which were used to marginalize and discriminate against different provinces of meaning and behavior for their sole purposive-rationale, i.e., economic gain for its own sake or capital accumulation, which psycho-logically had to be justified within the context of slavery (an institutional form for labor and capital accumulation), gender and racial discrimination, and heterosexism.

It is within this mechanical constitution of modernity and American society, as opposed to Habermas' "utopic" normative model or the determinism of the division of labor, that I attempt to understand the development or the social form black consciousness would take as constituted and directed by the black protestant male bourgeoisie within the two antinomic poles, class and race, of a permanent dialectic, which is at the heart of modern black American male representations of history.[9]

Thus, it follows from this claim that the discourse of the Protestant ethic within the discriminatory affects of class and race, as opposed to Habermas's rational communicative discourse, Marx's "find," i.e., "the capitalist mode of production is constituted by 'finding already there' (*vorfinden*) the elements which its structure combines[,]"[10] or the bourgeois ideology of "so-called primitive accumulation," set the social structural conditions (in the form of the American social structure or society)—[11] which were in turn recursively organized and reproduced by social actors in material practice—which gave rise to black American "practical-consciousness."[12] These "racial class" gendered Protestant values, as they were institutionalized and recursively organized in the laws (US Constitution) and other ideological institutions or apparatuses, i.e., the family, schools, Protestant churches, etc., of American society, to regulate social practices for the accumulation of capital or economic gain for its own sake, in other words, would have a long-term effect on the ways non-Protestant English and eventually non-European groups were interpellated, viewed, and dealt with, and how they would come to interpellate, view and deal with themselves in their relation to the means of producing capital or economic gain for its own sake (Hudson and Coukos, 2005; Cohen, 2002; Jones, 1971).[13]

Africans (an estimated 430,000 imported to North America during the whole period of the Atlantic Slave trade),[14] like Native Americans, and many poor whites, with other forms of orientation in the world distinct from the Protestant one of the American social structure and its agents, encountered or were brought (1619-1808) into this once marginalized Protestant worldview as marginalized forced laborers and indentured servants in order to satisfy the idea of "economic gain" in agricultural production expropriated from the "damned" that the new Protestant—economic—order ("slave-based plantation" agricultural capitalism)[15] proffered. In this ideologically economic driven new symbolic world, however, individual property rights were reconceptualized and elevated to a position sanctioned by divine authority and considered superior to all other rights, including the human rights and life of indigenous peoples, bonded laborers, and those who would eventually be bought as slaves (Smedley, 1999: 53). Thus, the institutional regulators (rich, white/Protestant, male landowners), given the need to maintain and reproduce the then agriculturally based economic stratified order of things among those "others" who did not subscribe to it, rationalized the labor requirements within what was already understood, the purposive-rationality of the Protestant ethic and the spirit of capitalism. By the time America was established as a nation-state in the late eighteenth-century this had already been done through the commodification of the Africans, who in the order of things, the bureaucratic social structural relations of white Protestantism, became the structurally differentiated perpetual "black," non-protestant, damned (i.e., commodity), who worked (as their property) *freely* for the predestined in order to maximize the rate of profit or economic gain.[16]

As the black nationalist thinker Maulana Karenga (1993) observes, several material factors made the enslavement of Africans for the increase of the rate of profit or economic gain in agricultural production more feasible and permanent then that of other marginalized "damned" groups such as Native Americans and poor white indentured-servants:

> The first factor was Africa's closeness to the Caribbean where plantations were set up early and where Africans were "seasoned," i.e., made manageable, and then re-exported. Secondly, Africans already had experience in large-scale agriculture with their own fields and European plantations in Africa, unlike the Native Americans who mainly hunted and gathered their food. Thirdly, Africans had relative immunity to European diseases due to long-term contact, whereas the Native Americans did not and were decimated at first by this.
>
> Fourthly, the practicality of African enslavement rested in their low escape possibilities as opposed to Native Americans and whites due to unfamiliarity with the land, high social visibility and lack of a nearby home base. Fifthly, there were no major political repercussions for the enslavement of Africans, unlike the Native Americans who had people here to retaliate and the whites whose enslavement would challenge the tenets of Christianity and the age of enlightenment and reason on which Europe prided itself.
>
> Finally, the basis of the American system of enslavement was in its justifiability in European racist thought. Although the enslavement of Africans was based in economic reasons, it also rested in racism as an ideology .... Racism as an ideology became a justification and encouragement for African enslavement (Karenga, 1993: 121-122).

These factors, however, were not perceived or conceived from a transcendental vantagepoint as Karenga's scientized material perspective implies. But their conjunctures were reasoned within what was already understood by those in power positions: rich, white, Protestant, men.[17] In other words, it is their rationalization through the prism of their Protestant ideology that would come to explain the social organization of the society, and the structural framework by which African American practical consciousness was constituted.

THE CONSTITUTION OF AFRICAN AMERICAN PRACTICAL CONSCIOUSNESS

The ever-increasing rationalization of the Protestant ethic by rich, white, Protestant men progressively elaborated and expanded on themes of Christian brotherhood, human rights, and the elevation of the good of the many over the privileges of the few, which were recursively organized and reproduced through the "secular" practice of bourgeois racial, gender, and patriarchal capitalism that would come to constitute American society. That is, the ideas of predestination through economic gain (as a sign of one's election or progress), duty, hard work, etc. justified the privileging of the good of the many (who were predestined to succeed—success being reflected in their economic gains or rate of profit) to have dominion over those who were not predestined, and who were, based on the structural (relational) logic of the former, backward, or damned. Those protestants and non-protestants who were not predestined, like their predestined counterparts, uncertain of their plight had to work hard in a particular calling for economic gain "as a sign;" while the enslaved, "damned," Africans, given their physical and behavioral differences, which were rationalized in relation to the symbolic signifiers of white Protestantism, were not quite human like the white protestants given their pigmentation, irrationalism, promiscuity, barbarity, carelessness, etc., and therefore had to work for them: class and status position or one's predestination being reflected in the rate of profit or economic gain obtained from the production of the "damned" or the laborers' of the predestined.

Rich, protestant, white, male landowners (the power elites of the society) the "enlightened" and "progressive" predestined, institutionalized or rationalized these Biblical, cultural, and entrepreneurial values into laws and practices, slave codes, miscegenation laws, systematic labor, capitalism, the individualism of civil rights and liberties, patriarchal family, republicanism, etc., embedded in pacts, agreements, the US and state constitutions, which came to bureaucratically structure the political economy of the material resource framework within which the society became ensconced, while at the same time structurally or relationally developing "blackness" and economic "class" as social categories (among others) for identity construction. More than anything else, this process of class and "racial"/national differentiation, counterposed as it was by equalization between predestined rich, white, Protestant, men, was responsible for the dialectical totality that gave rise to the black practical consciousness that would come to constitute and dominate modern American society.

Whereas in terms of Habermas's theoretical paradigm the protestant ideologies and capitalist practices of the society, which were institutionalized as laws and practices, are seen as the product of the "communicative action" of the varying groups (women, blacks, Jews, etc.) already existing within the society, my position is that the purposive-rationality of these laws was utilized through social institutions or "ideological apparatuses," i.e., the family, church, schools, organization of work (indentured servitude and slavery initially, consumerism and wage-labor, presently), etc., to condition or socialize (i.e., integrate) the masses—the constituting unit of the social structure—for the sole purpose of work or the reproduction of the American social relations of production, i.e., slavery in agricultural production. In other words, the embodiment of these laws and practices gave the masses and the power elites or institutional regulators their practical consciousness, while all other forms of social action, arrived at through the deferment of meaning in ego-centered communicative action, and the structurally differentiated were marginalized and discriminated against as unequal and "other" by rich, white, Protestant, men.

The Africans, ninety percent of whom could not read, as an introduced marginalized unit of the structure were "seasoned" in these same doctrines, slave codes, the Protestant churches (initially by white ministers, later on by native-born slaves), slavery, individual civil rights and liberties, etc. Unlike their literate non-protestant and protestant white counterparts, who could work hard and eventually—if predestined—become masters or what amounted to the same thing institutional regulators, as a structurally differentiated group the Africans had to accept their prescribed lowly conditions (slavery), given the fact that their physical difference, perpetual "otherness," in relation to white bourgeois (Patriarchal) Protestantism did not allow for their predestination or equality.

Thus their relationship with the power elites operated along a master/slave relationship, where the rich, white, Protestant males (masters) worked and reworked the ideas and practices of the protestant ethic on the one hand, and their terms and representations for the Africans' forms (soul-less, blacks, savages and barbarous, less intelligent and human than their white counterparts, ungodly, promiscuous, etc.) of being in the world, which they (rich, white, Protestant, heterosexual males) used to delimit their own form (godly, pious, obedient, pure, civilized, diligent, intelligent, etc.) of being in the world, on the other to reproduce the social relations of production, slavery.

Accordingly then, whereas it may have been the case that the Africans initially transported into this mechanical solidarity in the seventeenth and early part of the eighteenth centuries were different and heterogeneous, "others" with distinct practical consciousnesses, as a dominated deployable unit of the white protestant economic social relations of American society they became a homogeneous group, blacks (later differentially stratified along class lines and their adaptive responses to enslavement), prepared for one facet of life in the American social structure: "systematic labor" (Blassingame, 1972: 3) conditioned by the obedient work ethic of Protestantism.

In other words, Africans came from all over Africa,[18] and embodied different structurally determined subjective forms of being-in-the-world, which ranged from, rigid patriarchy, traditional Islamic practices, to matrilineal polygamous tribalism; by the nineteenth-century (1808), which marks the discontinuation of the African slave trade to the United States, these "other" forms of being-in-the-world were discriminated against and marginalized, within the American social structure, by native-born classified blacks, "the best of the house servants, mulattoes, artisans, and the educated free Negro from the North," who due to their freedom and privileges served as a reference group for the larger black community, and whites alike, who embodied and recursively organized and reproduced the Protestant cultural conditions of the society in their material practice.

So it is not that "in the process of acculturation the slaves made European forms serve African functions" (Blassingame, 1972: 17), as many of the representatives of the adaptive-vitality school contends; on the contrary, the majority of slaves had to choose, for their ontological security within the American social structure, between the European forms prescribed by power (whites and the best of the house servants, mulattoes, artisans, and the educated free Negro from the North) or the continual practice of their ontologically insecure "other" (African) forms of being in the world or any "other" fully visible, albeit discriminated against, "alternatives," which delimited the social structure.

This does not mean that nothing of Africa survived slavery because of the African's need to forsake African forms in order to move from being "other" in the new Protestant world setting. On the contrary, the suggestion is that different alternative categorical boundaries existed in the African community, and it was the "practical consciousness" of "the best of the house servants, mulattoes, artisans, and the educated free Negro from the North," which to a large extent rejected these African forms in order to be recognized by their white masters, that would come to represent and define black identity as these blacks became institutional regulators and the bearers of ideological and linguistic domination within the Protestant "class racism" of the dominant society (Winant, 2001).

AFRICANNESS IN RELATION TO WHITE PROTESTANT AMERICANISM

So, the structural logic here is that in the course of the development of American society, white, Protestant, males developed a series of laws and judicial rulings, "enframed" (Heidegger's term) by the cultural ideology of their protestant ethic, to define and represent the African (black cursed son of Ham, ungodly, licentious, emotional, irrational, uncivilized and barbaric, soul-less, etc.) situation in relation to that of whites' (white, godly, pious, obedient, pure, civilized, diligent, rational, etc.) in order to morally justify (given the internal contradiction between slavery and Christian brotherhood, human rights, etc.) and reproduce the integrative economic (Protestant) social relations of agricultural production (slavery) proffered by them as the power elites of the society. As the historian Vincent D. Harding (1981) highlights,

> Beginning in Virginia at the end of the 1630s, laws establishing lifelong [(*durante vita*)] African slavery were instituted.[19] They were followed by laws prohibiting black-white intermarriage, laws against the ownership of property by Africans, laws denying blacks all basic political rights (limited as they were among whites at the time). In addition, there were laws against the education of Africans, laws against the assembling of Africans, laws against the ownership of weapons by Africans, laws perpetuating the slavery of their parents to African children, laws forbidding Africans to raise their hands against whites even in self-defense.
>
> Then, besides setting up legal barriers against the entry of black people as self-determining participants into the developing American society, the laws struck another cruel blow of a different kind: they outlawed many rituals connected with African religious practices [(which were deemed heathenistic, lewd, licentious, etc.)], including dancing and the use of the drums. In many places they also banned African languages. Thus they attempted to shut black people out from both cultures, to make them wholly dependent neuters.
>
> Finally, because the religious and legal systems were so closely intertwined, everywhere in the colonies a crucial legislative decision declared that the Africans' conversion to Christianity [(the protestant type)] did not affect their enslavement . . . . Again, Virginia led the way: in 1667 its Assembly passed an act declaring that "the conferring of baptism doth not alter the condition of the person as to his bondage or freedome." Such laws freed many whites to do their Christian duty of evangelization and to reap the profit and the social standing of slave ownership at the same time (27).

Africans, who began arriving on the North American mainland "over more than a century preceding the War of Independence" (Gutman, 1976: 328), did not initially subscribe to this racial class ideological foundation, for they resisted enslavement and its institutionalization through ship mutinies prior to their arrival to the "New World;" guerilla wars; rebellions, the New York City Revolt in 1712, the Stono, South Carolina revolt in 1739, Gabriel Prosser revolt in 1800, Denmark Vesey conspiracy in 1822, the Nat Turner revolt in 1831, etc.—over 250 revolts are recorded in the US; suicide and infanticide; flights; and sabotage, i.e., breaking tools and destroying crops, shamming illness or ignorance, taking property, spontaneous, and planned strikes, work slow-downs, self-mutilation, arson, attacks on whites and poisoning of slaveholders and their families (Karenga, 1993; Bennett, 1982; Harding, 1981; Blassingame, 1972; Gutman, 1976; Aptheker, 1964; Franklin and Moss, 2000). These efforts, however, proved to be counter-productive to resisting subjugation, as they were incorporated by the white masters as evidence of the African's barbaric or savage disposition, the image of the African as unruly, rebellious, irrational, stupid, prone to thievery, destructive, sophomoric, licentious, and in turn used, relationally, to demonstrate to the slaves—during the "seasoning" process where the African learned Protestantism and its systematic work ethic—what was unacceptable behavior of a barbaric, black slave without religion.

As the historian John Blassingame (1972) points out in *The Slave Community*, "white ministers taught the slaves that they did not deserve freedom, that it was God's will that they were enslaved, that the devil was creating those desires for liberty in their breasts, and that runaways would be expelled from the church. Then followed the slave beatitudes: blessed are the patient, blessed are the faithful, blessed are the cheerful, blessed are the submissive, blessed are the hardworking, and above all, blessed are the obedient" (Blassingame, 1972: 62-63).[20] During the "seasoning" process, where the newly arrived Africans were forcefully taught, by the slave master, over-seers or native-born slaves, the language, religion, and work ethic or purposive-rationality of the American social structure, the majority of the early slaves, Stanley Elkins's Sambo, who worked intimately with their white masters, for their ontological security, incorporated these beliefs and practices, which they recursively organized and reproduced in their own material practices, and they became the structural terms, i.e., "good moral character, economic accumulation, temperance, industry, thrift, and learning," by which the larger slave community, which either maintained some element of their Africanisms in their material practices or developed a pathological-pathogenic form of the structural terms of the society given their relative isolation, was assessed (Elkins, 1959; Frazier, 1939, 1957; Stampp, 1956; Genovese, 1974).

In other words, with their very survival dependent upon following rules of conduct, which were sanctioned, many Africans acculturated or accommodated to the institution of slavery and incorporated the Protestant ethos (its work ethic, family organization, "white standards of morality," godliness, obedience, rationalism, etc.) into their way of being-in-the-world (Elkins, 1959; Frazier, 1939, 1957; Stampp, 1956; Genovese, 1974), which they and the dominant whites, as bearers of ideological domination, used to assess and determine the proper rules of conduct for the larger slave community.[21]

Those who did not accommodate were for the most part killed or brutally tortured until they did so. That is to say, as a deployable unit, i.e. black slaves, of the social structure, the social organization of family and cultural life in the majority of the African slave quarters became based on the ethical rules of the Protestant ethic against fully visible African ways of being-in-the-world, as demonstrated in the practices of newly arrived Africans or those who, through the constitution of alternative meanings and behaviors, either rejected the purposive-rationality of the American social structure, or sought to exercise them in "a national position"[22] of their own. This latter group of blacks included maroone communities of runaway slaves who attempted to exercise their African agential moments in the new world, and nationalist and conservative leading literate blacks such as Booker T. Washington, David Walker, Gabriel Prosser, Denmark Vesey, Nat Turner, Martin Delany, Henry Highland Garnet, etc., who, although they embodied the Protestantism of the social structure, sought not integration, like the majority of their bourgeois counterparts, but separation and black nationalism (Meier, 1963, 1966; Stuckey, 1987).

Consequently, the agential moments of those blacks who failed to exercise the purposive-rationality of the society, or rejected it in order to exercise them in "a national position" of their own, were discriminated against and marginalized by not only the slave owners and white overseers, but also those native-born acculturated liberal blacks, "the best of the house servants, mulattoes, artisans, and the educated free Negro from the North," who recursively organized and reproduced the purposive-rationality of the social structure, "the standard of good society," i.e., "temperance, industry, thrift, and learning . . . ," in their own material practices, for the sole purpose of integration in order to obtain equality of opportunity, distribution, and recognition in the society (Meier and Rudwick, 1966 [1976]: 127).[23]

What developed from all this was a class-color-caste system, i.e., a "caste in class," superordinate whites and subordinate blacks, perpetually subordinate, each dominated by the "predestined" class: blacks in relation to whites, in other words, emerged in the social structure of the "spirit of capitalism" as a caste (a racial class-in-itself as a result of "racial" structural differentiation) defined by their inherent fitness for slave labor to produce economic gain for their white masters, to a "caste in class" defined in relation to whites by those good obedient slaves (Stanley Elkins' Sambo, resulting from "class" structural differentiation), who embodied the protestant work ethic of the society for the sole purpose of integration or proving their predestination and those who did not because of their lack of "class" or need for separation.

This racial class social system became "reinforced" by the sociopolitical, religious, economic "legal system" (slavery and Jim Crow Segregation) in which the majority of the Africans followed the rules of conduct which were sanctioned by the master for the slave and himself (Drake, 1965: 3).[24] The majority of the slaves, given their "seasoning" in the American Protestant solidarity as a structurally differentiated racial class-in-itself, black slaves,[25] recursively organized and reproduced the rules of their masters, against the reproduced negative images of themselves by these same masters, to demonstrate their "predestination," or a sense of self-worth within the social structure among themselves: jumping over the broomstick to legalize marriages, an old English practice commonly used instead of church weddings, which were illegal for slaves; establishing traditional patriarchal nuclear families based on monogamy; establishing, as a result of segregation, Masonic lodges, churches, and mutual aid societies patterned after their white counterparts; demonstrating diligence in their work; instilling in their children a sense of Christian values;[26] black hymns; penning petitions for their liberation—the idea "that God granted temporal freedom, which man, without God's consent, had stolen away" (Blassingame,1972: 63),—based on reason and revelation as their white masters did against England; and a developing class distinction (also based on color, lighter blacks v, darker ones) between house, "mixed-bloods," Negroes and field slaves, the former, given their close ties to the slave owner and quasi-freedom, better off then the latter (Franklin, 1957; Karenga, 1993; Bennett, 1982; Harding, 1981; Blassingame, 1972; Gutman, 1976; Aptheker, 1964; Franklin and Moss, 2000).[27]

This acculturation for survival in essence eventually turned African consciousness among a *few* blacks, "favored" slaves, house slaves, artisans, "mixed-bloods," free colored population, who together numbered about 500, 000 at the outbreak of the Civil War, into an American, Protestant type. A practical consciousness amongst many blacks defined by their struggle for freedom, to exercise the purposive-rationality of the social structure and obtain class and status "based upon possession of money, education, and family background as reflected in distinctive styles of behavior" (Drake, 1965: 3), against the claim of "their inherent fitness for slavery and backwardness" which delimited the social structure and barred them from achieving economic gain and recognition.

THE BLACK PROTESTANT BOURGEOISIE
AND DOUBLE CONSCIOUSNESS

In sum, American society was founded on the rationales of rich, white, protestant men, the predestined master capitalist class. As the laws (US and State Constitutions) they enacted and institutionalized based on their biblical, cultural, and entrepreneurial practices "sought to provide legal sanction to the economic, political, and cultural domination and definition of the black captives from Africa by the whites from Europe, many of those laws at the same time, as part of the same objective, aimed at building a new fundamentally false solidarity between the upper and lower classes of the white population . . . " (Harding, 1981: 28). This racial ideology of white nationalism ("class racism") to justify the differentiation accorded to blacks amidst the universalism and equalization of the Protestant ethic and the spirit of capitalism was entirely compatible with the economic individualism of the Protestant ethic, and expanded positions of power to include, eventually, all white males (as the Constitution referred to "all persons," Africans before the passage of the Fourteenth Amendment did not count as persons—they were three-fifths of a person) antagonistic to blacks and their concerns.[28]

Blacks, consequently, shared in this structure of signification in that they were a discriminated against homogenized minority, "damned" black slave workers, whose behaviors, as prescribed by the white majority through institutions, the black church, slaves laws or codes, etc., had to reflect that of good, Christian servants (Sambo), as opposed to the barbarity associated with their Africanness or any other alternative forms, black maroon communities, black nationalist groups, black homosexuals, feminists, etc., of being-in-the-world arrived through the referment of meaning in ego-centered communicative action, lest their ontological security became threatened.

Be that as it may, it is not the case, as the adaptive-vitality school suggests, that as a structurally differentiated, discriminated against and marginalized group, blacks "made common choices rooted in a cumulative slave experience" in which other alternative (adjustments to enslavement) black forms of being-in-the American social structure, were incorporated into a larger community or value system (Gutman, 1976: 103,155).

The slave community, whose total slave population was of the order of 4 million by 1860,[29] was heterogeneous ("adaptation took many forms"), relationally defined by the different adjustments to enslavement and oppression within the larger slave community, which by the end of the Civil War was defined and determined by the adjustments of those blacks, who, for their ontological security, incorporated the Protestant rules of conduct or cultural structure of the larger American community, and therefore were accorded better social positions in the American caste system.

This group of blacks, "the black bourgeoisie" (E. Franklin Frazier's terms), marginalized and discriminated against all other black adaptive responses, which they deemed, or represented as, pathological-pathogenic in relation to their racialized bourgeois Protestantism, which they believed accorded them better equality of opportunity and recognition with their white counterparts (Frazier, 1939; 1957). In other words, their (black, protestant, men) purposive-rational or "practical consciousness" became defined, within two antinomic poles of race and class, by its bourgeois liberalism and racial nationalism: to recursively organize and reproduce the Protestant ethic in a racial nationalist position of their own in order to obtain equality of opportunity, distribution, and recognition for all blacks in the larger American society. This Du Boisian purposive-rationale was juxtaposed against the bourgeois conservatism of Booker T. Washington and the black nationalism of Henry Highland Garnett and Marcus Garvey, for examples, who sought to recursively organize and reproduce the Protestant ethic in a bourgeois separate and nationalist position.

The liberal black Protestant (male) bourgeois practical consciousness over time did not only become the dominant discourse in American society, but constantly had to (re) define itself in relation to the discursive practices of black feminists, whites, black conservatives, black nationalists, and the black underclass. Herein lies the origin of Du Boisian double consciousness. The ambivalent estrangement amongst the liberal black bourgeoisie is the nature of their own "class racism" and Du Bois's double consciousness, the struggle and desire to define and prove black self worth by obtaining equality of opportunity and recognition through their hard work, temperance, education, etc., against their derision for the discriminatory effects of the society, i.e., the racial and class marginalization they experience within the society due to their "other," African, forms of orientation in the world, which they also discriminate and define themselves against, but are used by their white counterparts to bar them from economic gain, equality, and recognition.

As Adolph Reed (1997) points out in his analysis of Du Bois's work *The Philadelphia Negro*, which gives an insight into Du Bois's view of the world: "[t]he strengths of Philadelphia's black community [(according to Du Bois)] are seen as those of its characteristics that most approximate the model of bourgeois [protestant] convention; the weaknesses that Du Bois identifies are those characteristics that most flaunt the conventional model. Broadly speaking, this model emphasizes, among other things: (1) monogamous nuclear family organization; (2) temperance and orderliness as behavioral principles, including thrift and internalization of disciplined work habits; (3) favorable disposition toward formal education and training in the ways of urban civilization; and (4) legitimation of class hierarchy within the racial community" (1997: 28).

So how is it that W.E.B. Du Bois and the later adaptive-vitality theorists intuit a double consciousness in the bicultural sense, amongst a distinct people whose sole aim was to "attain self conscious manhood, to merge his double self into a better and truer self," when institutions associated with their original African way of being were outlawed and replaced with new ideological apparatuses, the nuclear family, church, education, capitalism, etc., relationally intended to foster a distinct way of life (the Protestant ethic and its practices, the Spirit of Capitalism) as led by "the best of the house servants, [and] the educated free Negro from the North"? Du Bois, Reed argues, could do so only by relying on the neo-Lamarckian biological determinist outlook as mediated by the bourgeois ideology of nationalism, which dominated late nineteenth and early twentieth century social thought: Du Bois, like his white contemporaries, utilized the idea of race as a substance both biological and spiritual (i.e., the "souls" of black folk) to inscribe black folk in a temporal community (black nation within a nation) defined by their "doubleness." Today, given the refutation of this biological and ideological perspective (Balibar and Wallerstein, 1991 [1988]), many scholars (of the adaptive-vitality school) continue to articulate his position because of the cultural turn (which supplants race and nation) in analysis that concentrates on the physical body as the site for cultural meaning and signification irrespective of the practices the body exercises.

My structural understanding of the constitution of black American consciousness within the American Protestant solidarity dismisses both points, without, however, dismissing Dr. Du Bois's double consciousness construct, which has shaped contemporary understanding of black consciousness. That is, it is my thesis that even though the majority of black Americans, as a result of their attempt to "attain self conscious manhood" within one dominant structure of signification, developed multiple and diverse practices dominated by one dominant consciousness, the purposive-rationality of the protestant type and its practices, the spirit of capitalism, by which all other "alternative" black forms of being-in-the-world arrived at through the deferment of meaning in ego-centered communicative action were delimited and assessed, nevertheless the ambivalence that arises amongst this dominant group who are discriminated against as they seek economic gain and recognition in the society engenders a feeling of "doubleness," desire and derision. This has no basis in a different epistemology and or ontology in the discriminated against black, but is a result of having their presence serve as the "other" delimiting term which relationally defines the structure they attempt to be within, in order to deny their purposive-rationale, economic gain for its own sake and recognition. Hence, the "doubleness" Du Bois, as a paragon of this racial class, intuits and autobiographically articulates in *The Souls of Black Folk* is the ideological articulation of the liberal black bourgeoisie's ambivalence; their desire to achieve economic gain and recognition in the society, by exercising the agential moments of the society, and derision for that same society for its discriminatory practices which deny them the equality of opportunity, distribution, and recognition they seek for themselves and the black masses, who remain a permanent segregated underclass in the society because of the (racial class) discriminatory effects of the society.[30] The following chapter analyzes this ambivalence through an understanding of the constitution of W.E.B. Du Bois's own consciousness.

NOTES

1. The debate among historians of slavery has been the extent to which the nature (benevolent and patriarchal or oppressive and cruel) of the slave system, gave rise to black consciousness or identity. On the one hand, you have U.B. Philips, and to a less racist extent Eugene Genovese, Robert Fogel and Stanley Engerman, who argue that the slave system was benevolent and patriarchal, and blacks, given their childlike nature, accommodated to the system, where they were "civilized." On the other hand, E. Franklin Frazier, Kenneth Stampp, John Hope Franklin, Stanley Elkins, among many others, although they bear witness to blacks' accommodation to the system, nonetheless highlight the oppressiveness and brutality of the system and blacks' different forms of resistance to the system. I rather agree with August Meier (1966) that the system was both, and what accounts for the different perspectives are the time frames the historians are studying, the geographical locations, the origins of the Africans, and the plantation owners.

2. Joseph E. Holloway (1990) argues in his essay "The Origins of African-American Culture" that the West African ancestors of African Americans were culturally heterogeneous, which contradicts the cultural homogeneous assumption of many scholars such as Carter G. Woodson (1936), W.E.B. Du Bois (1939), and Lorenzo Turner (1949).

3. Stanley Elkin's *Slavery: a Problem in American Institutional and Intellectual Life* (1959), although somewhat flawed in its understanding of the slave institution through the eyes of the slaves, nonetheless, brilliantly captures the ambivalence between patriarchy and brutality.

4. See E. Franklin Frazier's *Black Bourgeoisie* (1957), Pp. 15.

5. Using a multivariate, locational-attainment approach in place of a segregation-index one, Alba et al (2000) found that "middle-income, suburban African Americans live in neighborhoods with many more whites than do poor, inner-city blacks" (545). Thus, corroborating the widely held position that differences (structural variables—class and status) in education, income and wealth, or property ownership, explain a substantial part of black-white segregation and identity formation (Clark, 1986; Galster, 1988; Wilson, 1987; Allen, 2000).

6. This is the process in socialization that Habermas refers to as "the colonization of the life-world."

7. This is what Etienne Balibar calls the "fictive ethnicity," "the community instituted by the nation-state" (Balibar and Wallerstein, 1991 [1988]: 96).

8. Weber's determinism is not an off-shoot of his idealism in "The Protestant Ethic and the Spirit of Capitalism." On the contrary, the iron cage thesis becomes determinist because of Weber's observation that protestant social actors reify their protestant ideals through the bureaucratization of society.

9. I focus on race and class because it is my position that these two poles have not been analyzed adequately together. bell hooks does a masterful job in looking at the roles of sex and gender in the constitution of black identity.

10. Karl Marx quoted in Balibar, Étienne (1968 [1970]: 283). "Elements for a Theory of Transition," pp.273-308. In *Reading Capital,* Louis Althusser and Étienne Balibar. London: NLB.

11. It is this sort of Polanyian (cultural) understanding, i.e., social relations "embedded" in the economic system, which guides my theoretical conception of the nature of the American ideological mechanical social structure, although, in my view, it was the rationalization of Protestant ideals as capitalist practices that resulted in Anglican, Puritan, and other Englishmen (a discriminated against minority in the Feudal social structure of the middle ages) recursively organizing and reproducing the culture to establish what would become the system/social integration we call the United States of America.

12 Stanley M. Elkins's *Slavery: A Problem in American Institutional and Intellectual Life* (1959), building on Frederick Jackson Turner's "frontier thesis," makes this capitalist argument. It is, however, my position that Elkins fails to account for the agency of the slaves within the American capitalist/paternalist social structure. See Herbert Gutman's *The Black Family in Slavery and Freedom, 1750-1925* (1976) for a critical critique of Elkins.

13. Jürgen Habermas sees this "colonization of the lifeworld" as a crisis; I see it as the basis of societal integration.

14. See Philip D. Curtin, *The Atlantic Slave Trade: A Census* (Madison, 1969), Pp.72-87.

15. See William Julius Wilson's *The Declining Significance of Race: Blacks and Changing American Institutions* (1978) for the economic and political dynamics involved in shaping southern institutions.

16. Whether on large plantations or small ones, all enslaved Africans in interaction with whites developed their practical consciousness by warring against the ways of the slavemaster and what they said the slaves, based on the fully visible behavior of newly arrived Africans, were.

17. In my structural understanding, the origins of American slavery, and its relation to the ideology of racism, is social structural. In other words, slavery in America was not an autonomous system which developed out "of the condition and status of seventeenth-century labor" (Elkins, 1968 [1972]), but, as Oscar and Mary F. Handlin imply (albeit for the Handlins their position was also in reference to economic conditions, whereas I am taking their reference to encompass a structuring ontology that

gives rise to institutions), "emerged rather from the adjustment to American conditions of traditional European institutions" (Handlins, 1950 [1972]: 23), which gave rise to the necessary conditions for the ever-increasing need for cheaper labor-power, which was in-turn rationalized or justified within the order of things, i.e., the Protestant ethic and the spirit of capitalism.

This synthesizing position, in the debate among historians of slavery as to the origins of racism in the United States, sides with Winthrop Jordan (1962 [1972]) who sees "both slavery and prejudice as species of a general debasement of the Negro", which stemmed, as Carl Degler (1959 [1972]) points out, from a stratifying, and discriminatory worldview bent on oppressing and exploiting (since the aim was extracting the most value out of labor for economic gain) the means it deemed necessary to meet or live out its end or ontology, i.e., economic gain for its own sake. In my view, accordingly, it is not enough to look at the material conditions, but on the contrary the structuring ontology by which the material condition is structured or recursively organized and reproduced.

18. See Joseph E. Holloway, "The Origins of African-American Culture," in "Africanisms in American Culture" (1990). Bloomington and Indianapolis: Indiana university Press, Pp. 2.

19. Massachusetts, founded by the Pilgrims, a Protestant sect, became the first colony (1641) to pass any enslavement laws.

20. It is no surprise that the seven major historic black denominations—the African Methodist Episcopal (A.M.E.) Church; the African Methodist Episcopal Zion (A.M.E.Z.) Church; the Christian Methodist Episcopal (C.M.E.) Church; the National Baptist Convention, U.S.A., Incorporated (NBC); the National Baptist Convention of America, Unincorporated (NBCA); the Progressive National Baptist Convention (PNBC); and the Church of God in Christ (COGIC)—that account for more than 80 percent of black religious affiliation in the United States are of the Baptist, Methodist, and Pentecostal Protestant variety. These Protestant churches with their high emotionalism, fervor, enthusiasm, and excitement, their revivalism, their excesses of sinning and high-voltage confessing (Bell, 1960: 103), has provided—for an illiterate mass prevented for a long time, on account of their immorality, lasciviousness, and heathenism, from partaking in the "thisworldly" affairs of the Protestant American social structure, derived from the intellectualism of traditional Protestantism—the means for access, via what is required for "otherworldly" existence, into the "thisworldly" affairs of the social structure.

In other words, for blacks, the Christianity of Methodism and Baptism served as a means to the Protestant ethic and the spirit of capitalism, the structuring structure, culture, that is American society. That is to say, the "Christianity that was spread among slaves during the First and Second Awakenings was an evangelical Christianity that stressed personal conversion through a deep regenerating experience, being born again. The spiritual journey began with an acknowledgement of personal sinfulness and unworthiness and ended in an emotional experience of salvation by God through the Holy Spirit. The rebirth meant a change, a fundamental reorientation in the approach to life" (Lincoln and Mamiya, 1990: 6)—becoming moral agents of the Protestant ethic in "this world" in order to have access to the "other world."

21. Some historians argue that the period prior to the cessation of the slave trade was more brutal and harsh than the period after the ban when slave masters relied almost completely on natural increase to reproduce the labor force. In my view, this distinction underestimates the degree to which the enslaved blacks' ontological security (the degree of brutality and oppressiveness) was attached to following plantation rules of conduct. In essence, my position is whether benign or brutal the general intent of the institution of slavery, as an ideological institution, was to inhibit the general autonomy and determine the agential moments of blacks. Just like the general intent of the organization of work in contemporary times is to maintain the capitalist social relations of production, and determine the agential moments of all wage laborers.

22. Martin Robinson Delany quoted in August Meier and Elliott Rudwick, *From Plantation to Ghetto* (New York, 1976), Pp. 151.

23. As August Meier and Elliott Rudwick (1966 [1976]) point out, this was the platform of the "Negro Convention Movement," which began in 1830 and met annually until the end of the century. A predominantly Northern phenomenon, "led and attended by the most distinguished leaders of the race—prominent ministers, physicians, lawyers, businessmen, and, after the Civil War, politicians . . . , the conventions provide illuminating insight into the thinking of articulate blacks on the problems facing the race" i.e., slavery and the discrimination and "indignities" of the free colored folks (126).

24. To do otherwise, that is practice their traditional African ways, would bring about cruel and unusual punishments, even death, considering that the African was, for the most part, under twenty-four hour surveillance in order to prevent insurrections. There is a debate amongst historians of slavery, who argue over the extent to which blacks within slavery had some form of autonomy. As can logically be deduced, the historians of the adaptive-vitality school (Blassingame, Gutman, Franklin, etc.) maintain that blacks were able to retain some of their African cultural heritage because they were to some extent autonomous; the historians of the pathological-pathogenic school (Elkins, Stampp, Genovese, etc.) argue to the contrary.

25. It should be noted that a debate lingers on regarding the origins of African spirituality. Given that the Africans were prevented from establishing any institutions to reproduce their ethos in the colonies, I rather agree with E. Franklin Frazier's (1957) understanding:

The most important institution which the Negro has built in the United States is the Negro church. Contrary to the claim of some students of the Negro that the Negro church was an African survival resurrected on American soil, the Negro church is a product of the American environment. The form of its organization and the character of its religious services were the result of the proselyting of Protestant missionaries, especially the Baptist and the Methodist missionaries. This does not mean that the Negro's peculiar experience in America did not contribute to the shaping of the institution. The influence of the Negro's experience in the building of his church is seen in the variations in the character of the Negro church, which reflect the extent of the Negro's education and isolation in American life and his economic and social status (87).

26. The character of the black family, during slavery, was so patterned after the institutional regulators of the American social structure, that today there is talk of its

disintegration resulting not from slavery, as E. Franklin Frazier (1939) proclaimed, but from post-World War II public policies, i.e., welfare, job relocations out of urban centers, etc., which has fostered female-headed households, teenage pregnancy, promiscuity, welfare dependency, out-of-wedlock births, etc. See, William Julius Wilson's (1987) *The Truly Disadvantaged*, and Herbert Gutman's (1976) *The Black Family in Slavery and Freedom*.

27. "As long as the slaves communed with whites [(and remained illiterate)], their religious instruction was circumscribed. The planters, in spite of their piety, insisted that their slaves not learn any of the potentially subversive tenets [(which whites themselves had used against their former masters, the English crown)] of Christianity (the brotherhood of all men, for instance)" (Blassingame, 1972: 61). Once they did, their quest for freedom became a fight for their "God" given rights.

28. See David R. Roediger's (1999) *The Wages of Whiteness: Race and the Making of the American Working Class*, as well as W.E.B. Du Bois's (1920) *Darkwater*, for an understanding of the impact race had in the construction of whiteness and its benefits.

29. Quoted in Hugh Tulloch, *The Debate on the American Civil War Era*, Manchester: Manchester University Press 1999, pp. 41.

30. This corroborates William Julius Wilson's (1978, 1987) thesis that race, as a determining factor for discrimination, is declining because the class factors of black existence are more relevant in discriminating against them than race, although, these class factors become conflated with the racial stereotypes, promiscuity, laziness, dependent, female-headed families, out-of-wedlock births, etc., which determined the black experience during slavery.

My point, in evoking Wilson, is to highlight two points in regard to this conflation: first, the fact that outside of the physical differences, only class distinction divides blacks from mainstream America (black and white middle-class groups). That is, once upper mobility is obtained, through education and professional occupations, there is no distinct black identity or consciousness. In fact, Wilson and others have pointed out that blacks, who become upwardly mobile through the attainment of higher education, assume acceptable mainstream behaviors. Which brings us to the second point, the response of Blacks to this conflation: assimilated blacks, like Wilson, proffer public policy agendas, for the "social isolation" of the black underclass, which will foster mainstream values, i.e., job creations, education etc, over those welfare policies that exacerbate the culture of poverty, i.e., promiscuity, out-of-wedlock families, teenage pregnancy, dependency, female headed households, etc., which have developed as a result of attempting to exercise a reified consciousness focused on material accumulation in a material resource depleted environment. Which again proves that black consciousness simply is the degree to which blacks attempt to exercise the reified consciousness of the American social structure, i.e., the protestant ethic, and its discursive praxis, the spirit of capitalism.

Chapter Three

On the Interpretation of Du Bois's Double Consciousness

W.E.B. Du Bois, early on in his life 885-1910), saw the historical situation of the African living in America as leading to a "double consciousness." In order to better understand this construct, this chapter subsumes the historical development of Du Bois's consciousness and his early understanding of consciousness formation within my structural understanding.

Adolph Reed, in *W.E.B. Du Bois and American Political Thought: Fabianism and the Color Line*, points out that the autobiographical construct proceeded from the conventions of neo-Lamarckian social science, which stressed the belief in inheritance of acquired characteristics and hierarchical essentialism, which dominated late nineteenth and early twentieth-century social thought (Reed, 1997: 119-121). Thus, Du Bois's conclusion in *The Souls of Black Folk* that the experience of black Americans is the strivings of two thoughts, one African and the other white American, within one dark body is a direct result of this neo-Lamarckian framework as mediated by the concept of nation on his reasoning, the backward uncivilized black American nation having one thought given the "sensuous, tropical love" of their "black blood," which stands in vivid contrast to the Protestantism, "cool and cautious New England reason," of white civilized America.

My reading substantiates Reed's position without, however, dismissing the construct. In fact, it is my position that the construct is not a reference to biculturalism as Du Bois understood and applied to blacks in general. On the contrary, it is meaningful in relation to the dominant interpretive community Du Bois represented in the black community, mainly the liberal black bourgeoisie or middle class. Du Bois's construct highlights his ambivalence, which is rooted in his class (or lack thereof) position, toward the American nation-state, as opposed to offering an accurate depiction of black American practical consciousness.

DU BOISIAN DOUBLE CONSCIOUSNESS

Scholars since the 1960s, the "radical" era out of which contemporary notions of African-American identity as Du Boisian "double consciousness" took shape (Allen, 1992), have described the dualism in various ways: 1) the traditional assimilationist/nationalist readings, coming out of the humanities (adaptive-vitality school), which emphasize the theory as representing the "twoness" of black cultural identity, a la Reed; and (2) the more contemporary positivist readings which refute the latter position either on the grounds that a strict reading of the metaphor describes a form of "alienation" rather than two opposing modes of identity (Allen, 1992, 2002; Holt, 1990), or repudiate it on account of the lingering biological conception of race that persists beneath the sociohistorical attempt of Du Bois and that of the assimilationist/nationalist readings (Appiah, 1985; Reed, 1997; Crouch, 1993).

In the traditional assimilationist/nationalist readings, through which many scholars and the general public have come to interpret and understand double consciousness, the argument is that Du Bois's reference speaks to the distinct bicultural nature of black life. Hence, the historian August Meier (1959, 1963) advanced the thesis that the construct reflects Du Bois's own "ambivalent" ideological struggles (i.e., "paradox") between racial separatism and democratic rights for the "Negro" as an American. In fact, in his work *Negro Thought in America*, Meier dubbed Du Bois an "equalitarian who apparently believed in innate racial differences" (1963: 206).

Most subsequent assimilationist/nationalist interpretations of the theory share Meier's basic interpretation but view his dubious take on Du Bois's "innate racial differences" as representing the "real" and appealing choice blacks must make between two opposing cultural identities: "assimilated Americanness" or "unassimilated Negroness" (Early, 1993: xx). In other words, this position assumes, as Dickson D. Bruce's essay, "W.E.B. Du Bois and the Idea of Double Consciousness," contends,

> by double consciousness Du Bois referred most importantly to an internal conflict in the African American individual between what was 'African' and what was "American." It was in terms of this ... sense that the figurative background to "double consciousness" gave the term its most obvious support, because for Du Bois the essence of a distinctive African consciousness was its spirituality, a spirituality based in Africa but revealed among African Americans in their folklore, their history of patient suffering, and their faith (1992: 301).

In light of these readings and critiques, some scholars, such as David Levering Lewis for example, comment that the genius of the "double consciousness" metaphor is that it transcends the assimilationist/nationalist debate or conflict by conceiving the "destiny of the race . . . as leading neither to assimilation nor separatism but to proud, enduring hyphenation" (Lewis, 1993: 281). "A biracial, bicultural state of being in the world," Bernard W. Bell posits, which signifies "a dynamic epistemological mode of critical inquiry for African Americans" (Bell, 1996: 96). A view shared by the more positivist oriented scholar, Richard L. Allen, whose sociological study, *The Concept of Self: A Study of Black Identity and Self-Esteem*, departs from Du Bois's construct (Allen, 2001: 30).

For the most part, these assimilationist/nationalist or biculturalist readings of double consciousness, assume an external validity that underscores the general contemporary understanding of the text and its prescience in capturing the dualistic nature of black consciousness. Du Boisian biographer Arnold Rampersad (1976: 74-75) comments, "[t]he 'souls' of the title is a play on words, referring to the 'twoness' of the black American," which calls "for the recognition" of their "dignity and separate identity." Eric J. Sundquist argues, "*The Souls of Black Folk* established the coherence of African American culture as a set of values and expressions that were not annihilated by slavery but nurtured by its 'voice of exile'" (1996:16).

For more nationalistic thinking scholars, the book exhibits a tension between the black Americans' national (American) and racial (black or African) identities. Reasoning along these lines, Houston Baker (1972) and Manning Marable (1986) suggest that *Souls* moves between a Victorian elitism and an appreciation for the distinct "folk culture" of the black Masses. Paul Gilroy (1993) and Bernard W. Bell (1985,1996), like many other "post-segregation-era" academics turned "public-intellectuals" (Cornel West and Henry Louis Gates also come to mind) who have appropriated "Du Bois's construct for a purely academic program" (Reed, 1997: 96), i.e., to formulate and articulate the "epistemological mode of critical inquiry" which stems from the African Americans' synthesized "double consciousness," see *Souls* as an articulation of Du Bois's own attempt to synthesize his "doubleness" (Dutch and African ancestry)—an experience which he extrapolates-from to explain African American racial and ethnic difference and their keen or critical insight (i.e., "second-sight") into "modernity" resulting from this peculiarity.

More recently, in contradistinction to these traditional readings of Du Boisian "double consciousness" "as a reference to and a confirmation of the existence of ambiguities and vacillations between assimilationist and nationalist tendencies in African American life" (Allen, 1992: 261), Ernest Allen Jr. argues that any suggestion that Du Bois's construct speaks to an internal struggle amongst the members of the tiny, educated black elite, who are "torn between the [(cultural)] values of, on the one hand, upper-or middle-class whites and, on the other, those black sharecroppers, domestics, and other working people (that is, as one might say today, between a Eurocentric and an Afrocentric cultural orientation), is, quite simply, a proposition unsupported" (Allen, 2002: 220) by a closer reading of Du Bois's own evidence in *The Souls of Black Folk*. For, according to Allen, the use of culture in traditional readings of Du Boisian double consciousness would be unfamiliar to Du Bois; such an interpretation is not in line with his reasoning at the time that he penned *The Souls*.

Consequently, it is this recognized (Du Bois, 1940; Meier, 1963; DeMarco, 1983; Appiah, 1985; Crouch, 1993; Reed, 1997)"neo-Lamarckian" interpretation of "double consciousness," which contains the assimilationist/nationalist approach with the notion of an authentic "blackness," and which has dominated social science literature on understanding black racial identity and self-consciousness, then and now, I find problematic. It continues Du Bois's usage of the construct to highlight its prescience in explaining black American identity or consciousness, without re-conceptualizing the metaphor and black consciousness in general, given Du Bois's reliance on nineteenth-century racial sciences and national ideology to develop the theoretical metaphor.

DOUBLE CONSCIOUSNESS RECONSIDERED

My analysis of this "doubleness" construction of black consciousness is a result of the refutation of late nineteenth and twentieth century racial and national ideology, a turn Du Bois also took toward the end of his life with his conversion from pan-African nationalism to a Marxist historical materialist view of the world:

> There are no races, in the sense of great, separate, pure breeds of men, differing in attainment, development, and capacity. There are great groups,—now with common history, now with common interests, now with common ancestry; more and more common experience and present interest drive back the common blood and the world today consists, not of races, but of the imperial commercial group of master capitalists, international and predominantly white; the national middle classes of the several nations, white, yellow, and brown, with strong blood bonds, common languages, and common history; the international laboring class of all colors; the backward, oppressed groups of nature-folk, predominantly yellow, brown, and black (Du Bois, 2003 [1920]: 115; 1968).

The question I pose, as a result of this turn, is what then of the souls or consciousness of black folk as they strove to be within the world constituted through one singular ideologically constructed order of reality (i.e., the Protestant ethic and the spirit of capitalism "of the imperial commercial group of master capitalists") defined relationally and differentially by their relation to the means of production and to other fully visible forms of being-in-the-world or categorical boundaries with their own power elites? In answering this question, I do not dismiss the early Du Bois autobiographical sense of doubleness grounded in late nineteenth and early twentieth century racial and national ideology; I simply question its nature and origin.

As I have demonstrated in the sociohistorical outline of black American history in the previous chapter, this striving or struggle to be in the kingdom of culture, which Du Bois suggests characterizes the souls of black folk, did not and does not take place between two distinct and contradictory practical consciousnesses, one black and one white within their dark bodies, as the adaptive-vitality school building on the early writings of Du Bois suggests.

Instead, my argument, in building on the structural approach of the pathological-pathogenic school, is that Africans had to construct and constructed their sense of "being-in-the-world," their practical consciousness, in a singular, ideological "mechanical and relational"[1] totality (the protestant ethic and the spirit of capitalism) "embodied in institutions and apparatuses" defined through, what Homi Bhabha calls, "disavowal," the production of discriminatory identities that secure the 'pure' and original identity of authority; in my understanding of consciousness as practical consciousness, the structural (re)production of fully visible "other" practical consciousnesses within and by (its power elites) a dominant social order as "discriminatory identities that [relationally] secure the 'pure' and original identity [(practical consciousness)] of authority."

In this framework, as we will see through an analysis of Du Bois's early thoughts and actions, I am suggesting that the doubleness of the discriminated against constituted subject of the social structure, which Du Bois intuits in *The Souls*, should not be interpreted as a reference to biculturalism, but instead, it should be interpreted as a general description of the ambivalence, which arises in the structurally differentiated discriminated against at the moment of antagonism (the moment of discrimination) between themselves and authority as they attempt to recursively organize and reproduce the incorporated "pure" identity of authority as an "other" or outsider.

Although this marginalization as a hybrid "other," and the moment of antagonism (between discriminator and the discriminated against), possesses the potentiality for diversity, given that, as the psychoanalytically minded Bhabha puts it, "the presence of power is revealed as something other than what its rules of recognition assert," socially constructed as opposed to its projected naturalism, in the case of the majority of black Americans, as I have demonstrated in the previous chapter, the result was cultural homogenization. The majority of Africans, as a "class-in-itself" led by the best of the house-servants, free Negroes from the north, and mulattoes, warred against the "other" fully visible image of themselves practiced among a minority underclass created by the relational bourgeois racist and capitalist logic of those in power in the social structure, for the incorporation of "the 'pure' and original identity of authority," assessing as "other" blacks who chose to reject or failed at reproducing the "pure" identity of power in terms of the practical consciousness (structural variables—class and status) of the dominating American capitalist bourgeois social order.

Thus, the ambivalence, the desire to prove their self worth in the society and reject the contempt to which they are subject, which arose and arises out of discrimination and exploitation, is the essence of Du Bois's, as a member of this former class, own "doubleness" and "double consciousness" construct.[2] Let us look at this beginning with Du Bois's practical consciousness and extrapolating our conclusions to present day black American consciousness.

THE EARLY THOUGHTS AND ACTIONS OF W.E.B. DU BOIS

William Edward Burghardt Du Bois (February 23, 1868-August 27, 1963) was born to Alfred Du Bois and Mary Silvina Burghardt Du Bois one year after the Fourteenth Amendment was ratified, and added to the US Constitution. After graduating from Fisk University (1888), Du Bois earned a bachelor's degree from Harvard, studied abroad in Berlin, and returned to Harvard where he became the first black American to earn a Ph.D. He went on to teach at Wilberforce University in Ohio, the University of Pennsylvania, and Atlanta University where he established the department of sociology. The descendant of free people of color from the Caribbean and the North, Du Bois knew nothing of Africa or the South, until his Fisk years, and his encounters with discrimination and racism stems from the racial biases of his Protestant community toward the Scots-Irish, and his marginalization by a female schoolmate when he was in grade school.

Hence, born and raised in the predominantly white Protestant community of Great Barrington, Massachusetts, Du Bois, was, as Cornel West (1996) points out,

> ... first and foremost a black New England Victorian seduced by the Enlightenment ethos and enchanted with the American Dream. His interpretation of the human condition—that is, in part, his idea of who he was and could be—was based on his experiences and, most importantly, on his understanding of those experiences through the medium of an Enlightenment worldview that promoted Victorian strategies in order to realize an American optimism. . . . Like many of

> the brilliant and ambitious young men of his time, he breathed the intoxicating fumes of "advanced" intellectual and political culture. . . . [This intellectual and political culture, however,] precluded his access to the distinctive black tragicomic sense and black encounter with the absurd. He certainly saw, analyzed, and empathized with black sadness, sorrow, and suffering. But he didn't feel it in his bones deeply enough, nor was he intellectually open enough to position himself alongside the sorrowful, suffering, yet striving ordinary black folk. Instead, his own personal and intellectual distance lifted him above them even as he addressed their plight in his progressive writings. Du Bois was never alienated by black people—he lived in black communities where he received great respect and admiration. But there seemed to be something in him that alienated ordinary black people. In short, he was reluctant to learn fundamental lessons about life—and about himself—from them. Such lessons would have required that he—at least momentarily—believe that they were or might be as wise, insightful, and "advanced" as he; and this he could not do (58).

Du Bois could not see that "ordinary black people were or might be as wise, insightful, and advanced as he" precisely because he was an agent of the Protestant ethic and his times and therefore saw "ordinary black people," whose equality to whites he felt "lay in excellence in accomplishment" (Du Bois, 1968: 75), and their practical consciousness as a backward "other," held back not because of their racial difference, "innate love of harmony and beauty," but by "race prejudice." This "racial prejudice," unlike the majority of "ordinary black people," he was for the most part able to avoid growing up in the northern town of Great Barrington where he was socialized. As Du Bois observes of his own upbringing,

> In general thought and conduct I became quite thoroughly New England. It was not good form in Great Barrington to express one's thoughts volubly, or to give way to excessive emotion. We were even sparing in our daily greetings. There was on the street only a curt "good morning" to those whom you knew well and no greetings at all from others. I am quite sure that in a less restrained and conventional atmosphere I should have easily learned to express my emotions with far greater and more unrestrained intensity; but as it was I had the social heritage not only of a New England clan but Dutch taciturnity. This was later reinforced and strengthened by inner withdrawals in the face of real and imagined discriminations. The result was that I was early thrown in upon myself. I found it difficult and even unnecessary to approach other people and by that same token my own inner life perhaps grew the richer; but the habit of repression often returned to plague me in after years, for so early a habit could not easily be unlearned. The Negroes in the South, when I came to know them, could never understand why I did not naturally greet everyone I passed on the street or slap my friends on the back (Du Bois, 1968: 93).

Thus, Du Bois, who experienced *little* race prejudice in his formative years (1868-1885) where he attended an all white Episcopalian church and school, like the rest of the black bourgeoisie during his lifetime, "the best of the house servants, [and] the educated free Negro from the North," who together numbered about 500, 000 "at the outbreak of the Civil War," became, given his socialization, a bourgeois agent of the Protestant ethic whose understanding of the world and "others" was based on: "(1) monogamous nuclear family organization; (2) temperance and orderliness as behavioral principles, including thrift and internalization of disciplined work habits; (3) favorable disposition toward formal education and training in the ways of urban civilization; and (4) legitimation of class hierarchy within the racial community" (Reed, 1997: 28). Unlike many of his white and black Protestant bourgeois contemporaries, however, he does not view "the Negroes in the South," i.e., "ordinary black people," whom he saw as being distinct from his "New England and Dutch social heritage," in the structurally derogatory and antithetical Protestant terms (i.e., lazy, promiscuous, emotional, disorderly, etc.) of the larger white society; instead, "when he first came to know them," on a return trip from New Bedford, Massachusetts with his grandfather in 1883, Du Bois celebrates their distinctiveness, i.e., "otherness:"[3]

> ...I viewed with astonishment ten thousand Negroes of every hue and bearing, saw in open-mouthed astonishment the whole gorgeous gamut of the American Negro world; the swaggering men, the beautiful girls, the laughter and gaiety, the unhampered self-expression. I was astonished and inspired. I apparently noted nothing of poverty or degradation, but only extraordinary beauty of skin-color and utter equality of mien, with absence so far as I could see of even the shadow of the line of race (Du Bois, 1968: 99).

In songs and religious practices, Du Bois, when he attends Fisk for college in 1885, also becomes aware of that "unhampered self-expression" of blackness which made the Negro "community a world" distinct from his Puritan community:

> I heard the Negro folksong first in Great Barrington, sung by the Hampton Singers. But that was second-hand, sung by youth who never knew slavery. I now heard the Negro songs by those who made them and in the land of their American birth. It was in the village into which my country school district filtered of Saturdays and Sundays. The road wandered from our rambling log-house up the stony bed of a creek, past wheat and corn, until we could hear dimly across the fields a rhythmic cadence of song—soft, thrilling, powerful, that swelled and died sorrowfully in our ears. I had never seen a Southern Negro revival. To be sure, we in Berkshire were not perhaps as stiff and formal as

they in Suffolk, of olden time; yet we were very quiet and subdued, and I know not what would have happened those clear Sabbath mornings had someone punctuated the sermon with a scream, or interrupted the long prayer with a loud Amen!

And so most striking to me, as I approached the village and the little plain church perched aloft, was the air of intense excitement that possessed that mass of black folk. A sort of suppressed terror hung in the air and seemed to seize them—a pythian madness, a demoniac possession, that lent terrible reality to song and word. The black and massive form of the preacher swayed and quivered as the words crowded to his lips and flew at us in singular eloquence. The people moaned and fluttered, and then the gaunt-cheeked brown woman beside me suddenly leaped straight into the air and shrieked like a lost soul, while round about came wail and groan and outcry, and a scene of human passion such as I had never conceived before (Du Bois, 1968: 120).

Thus, at Fisk, Du Bois, through their emotionalism, spiritualism, and music, encounters "a" black, underclass, world, which differed from his middle class upbringing, and embraces it,

I have called my community a world, and so its isolation made it. There was among us but a half-awakened common consciousness, sprung from common joy and grief, at burial, birth or wedding; from a common hardship in poverty, poor land and low wages; and, above all, from the sight of the Veil that hung between us and Opportunity (Du Bois, 1968:120).

"The Fisk years" (1885-1888), as Julius Lester (1971) suggests, "were the beginning. He came there an American looking for blackness; he left, having become aware of that blackness" (12):

I forgot, or did not thoroughly realize, the curious irony by which I was not looked upon as a real citizen of my birth-town, with a future and a career, and instead was being sent to a far land among strangers who were regarded as (and in truth were) "mine own people" (Du Bois, 2003 [1920]: 42).

So I came to a region where the world was split into white and black halves, and where the darker half was held back by race prejudice and legal bonds, as well as by deep ignorance and dire poverty. But facing this was not a lost group, but at Fisk a microcosm of a world and a civilisation in potentiality. Into this world I leapt with enthusiasm. A new loyalty and allegiance replaced my Americanism: hence-forward I was a Negro (Du Bois, 1986 [1968]: 108).

The net result of the Fisk interlude was to broaden the scope of my program of life, not essentially to change it; to center it in a group of educated Negroes, who from their knowledge and experience would lead the mass. I never for a moment dreamed that such leadership could ever be for the sake of the educated group itself, but always for the mass. Nor did I pause to enquire in just what ways and with what technique we would work—first, broad, exhaustive knowledge of the world; all other wisdom, all method and application would be added unto us.

In essence I combined a social program for a depressed group with the natural demand of youth for "Light, more light" (Du Bois, 1986 [1968]: 123).

Clearly, in his early thoughts and actions, Du Bois (as these quotes demonstrate) is aware of an overt difference between his upbringing, demeanor, and overall outlook on life, which he deems Americanism, and "the unhampered self-expression" of a group of strangers in the South who were regarded as his own people. Why and how, then, is "double consciousness" in *The Souls of Black Folk* (1903) the sign of the racial and national distinctiveness of black culture and character, biculturalism, characterized by Du Bois's Americanism and this "unhampered self-expression," i.e., "emotionalism" and "spiritual and musical ideals"? Why is the "unhampered self-expression" of black folk not merely the dissolution and reformulation of Du Bois's Americanism, among a segregated and "isolated" minority (i.e., "depressed group"), hampered by the material conditions (i.e., "hardship in poverty," "poor land and low wages," "race prejudice and legal bonds," and "ignorance and dire poverty"), "barbarism," and relational logic of the South or that same Americanism?

DU BOIS'S DOUBLE CONSCIOUSNESS

The answer to these two questions is simple. Du Bois, the father of pan-African bourgeois nationalism led by the "Talented Tenth" of the race, by the time he publishes *The Souls of Black Folk* (1903), which is a collection of fourteen essays previously published during the early years of his life, has both a racial deterministic and sociocultural view of race mediated by the late nineteenth and early twentieth century concept of nation, which turned the "spiritual idealism and musical style" of the isolated black, underclass, community into their African "innate love of harmony and beauty" which relationally made them racially and nationally distinct from their white counterparts:

> But while race differences have followed mainly physical race lines, yet no mere physical distinctions would really define or explain the deeper differences, the cohesiveness, and continuity of these groups. The deeper differences are spiritual, psychical, differences—undoubtedly based on the physical, but infinitely transcending them. The forces that bind together the Teuton nations are, then, first, their race identity and common blood; secondly, and more important, a

common history, common laws and religion, similar habits of thought and a conscious striving together for certain ideals of life. The whole process which has brought about these race differentiations has been a growth, and the great characteristic of this growth has been the differentiation of spiritual and mental differences between great races of mankind and the integration of physical differences.... Here, it seems to me, is the reading of the riddle that puzzles so many of us. We are Americans, not only by birth and by citizenship, but by our political ideals, our language, our religion. Farther than that our Americanism does not go. At that point we are Negroes, members of a vast historic race that from the very dawn of creation has slept, but half awakens in the dark forests of its African fatherland. We are the first fruits of this new nation, the harbinger of that black tomorrow which is yet destined to soften the whiteness of the Teutonic today. We are that people whose subtle sense of song has given America its only American music, its only American fairy tales, its only touch of pathos and humor amid its money-getting plutocracy. As such, it is our duty to conserve our physical powers, our intellectual endowments, our spiritual ideals; as a race we must strive by race organization, by race solidarity, by race unity to the realization of that broader humanity which freely recognizes differences in men, but sternly deprecates inequality in their opportunities of development (Du Bois, 1971 [1897]: 179-183).

This 1897 passage, published the same year as "Of Our Spiritual Strivings" where Du Bois first conceptualized the double consciousness construct, highlights Du Bois's nineteenth-century racial understanding of consciousness formation as mediated by the concepts of race and nation, which he would apply to his understanding of who he was and who the rest of black America was. Du Bois, as his autobiographies read, was completely embroiled in the "white Americanism" of Great Barrington, albeit racially distinct because of his physical difference, "black blood," until he goes to Fisk where he encounters the "spiritual" and "psychical" strivings of his "undoubtedly" physical difference—"Then of course, when I went South to Fisk, I became a member of a closed racial group with rites and loyalties, with a history and a corporate future, with an art and philosophy." Building on late nineteenth and early twentieth century notions of racialism and nationalism, which focused on drawing boundaries between nation-states and racial bodies that marked national "insiders" and "outsiders," Du Bois utilized the idea of race as a substance both biological and spiritual (the "souls" of black folk) to inscribe black folk in a temporal community, black nation, defined by its "doubleness," American and Negro. The former characterized by its civilization and "enlightenment" ethos, the latter by its emotionalism and spiritualism. In other words, whites, the Teuton nation, were characterized by their rationality and temperance, and blacks, southern blacks, were characterized by their emotionalism, spiritualism, and musical style.

Alienated from both groups—the larger society because of his "black blood," and black America because his education and "social heritage" detached him from their "unfortunate" experiences—however, Du Bois ambivalently sought refuge in uplifting the latter (to his status position) in order to voice what he saw, through the prism of race and nation, as their distinct (racial and national) voice or soul, i.e., religiosity and music (stemming from Africa), without bleaching it "in a flood of white Americanism," i.e., his Enlightenment (status) ethos:

> Here, then, is the dilemma, and it is a puzzling one, I admit. No Negro who has given earnest thought to the situation of his people in America has failed, at some time in life, to find himself at these crossroads; has failed to ask himself at some time, "What, after all, am I? Am I an American or am I a Negro? Can I be both? Or is it my duty to cease to be a Negro as soon as possible and be an American? If I strive as a Negro, am I not perpetuating the very cleft that threatens and separates black and white America? Is not my only possible practical aim the subduction of all that is Negro in me to the American? Does my black blood place upon me any more obligation to assert my nationality than German, or Irish or Italian blood would?" . . . [I]t is our duty to conserve our physical powers, our intellectual endowments, our spiritual ideals; as a race we must strive by race organization, by race solidarity, by race unity to the realization of that broader humanity which freely recognizes differences in men, but sternly deprecates inequality in their opportunities of development (Du Bois, 1971 [1897]: 182-183).

Clearly, the late nineteenth and early twentieth century "discourse of blood, skin colour and cross-breeding" (Balibar, 1991: 207) concealed Du Bois's ambivalence, and shaped his understanding of his "black identity" as a double consciousness, a bicultural form of being-in-the-world that distinguished and alienated him from *both* black and white America:

> After the Egyptian and Indian, the Greek and Roman, the Teuton and Mongolian, the Negro is a sort of seventh son, born with a veil, and gifted with second-sight in this American world,—a world which yields him no true self-consciousness, but only lets him see himself through the revelation of the other world. It is a peculiar sensation, this double-consciousness, this sense of always looking at one's self through the eyes of others, of measuring one's soul by the tape of a world that looks on in amused contempt and pity. One ever feels his twoness,—an American, a Negro; two souls, two thoughts, two unreconciled strivings; two warring ideals in one dark body, whose dogged strength alone keeps it from being torn asunder.
> The history of the American Negro is the history of this strife,—this longing to attain self conscious manhood, to merge his double self into a better and truer self. In this merging he wishes neither of the older selves to be lost. He would

not Africanize America, for America has too much to teach the world and Africa. He would not bleach his Negro soul in a flood of white Americanism, for he knows that Negro blood has a message for the world. He simply wishes to make it possible for a man to be both a Negro and an American, without being cursed and spit upon by his fellows, without having the doors of Opportunity closed roughly in his face (Du Bois, 1995 [1903]: 43-47).

As is clearly outlined from this often-quoted conception of "double consciousness" in *The Souls of Black Folk*, Du Bois's take is not that the black American is only an American (upper middle class sensibility) hampered by the poverty and racial prejudice of the South or the "other world," as I am suggesting and to which Du Bois admittedly alludes to in his later (1968) autobiographical writings; on the contrary, in *The Souls of Black Folk* he is suggesting that the Black American's consciousness is divided between two distinct epistemologies and ontologies—" two souls, two thoughts"—one African (Negro), with its own "innate messages" stemming from his "Negro blood," and the other white (American).

If Du Bois by the time he penned *The Souls of Black Folk* has fully transcended the racial and national ideology of the late nineteenth and early twentieth century, what is the role of this talk about 'blood' and 'Teuton' nation? This question is a moot point. For the problem for Du Bois in the above-mentioned passages is not the concept of blood and nation as the basis for the constitution of black consciousness, which he clearly accepts. The problem for Du Bois is the "peculiar sensation;" that the "African World" is structurally revealed to the African "through the revelation of the other world," which "looks on in amused contempt and pity" and prevents the "Negro" from reconciling their "twoness," given the juxtaposition of the two "physical" worlds in diametrical opposition to one another (White is civilized, Black is barbaric, etc.).

It is this ambivalent estrangement or strife, the desire "to attain self conscious manhood" and reject the contempt to which they are subject, produced by the society's structural ("class racism") differentiation, that Du Bois captures with his racialized and nationalized double consciousness construct. The construct, as such, does not, however, without relying on their "innate love of harmony and beauty," articulate the sociohistorical nature of all black practical consciousness or identity. It instead highlights the liberal bourgeois (class) basis of the construct as supplemented by race: the desire of the liberal black bourgeoisie to seek equality of opportunity, distribution, and recognition in the American capitalist social milieu amidst their contempt for that milieu because they are "cursed and spitted" upon and prevented from achieving that equality or integration. It is this purposive-rationale Du Bois captures with his construct against the conservative bourgeois economism of Booker T. Washington, who sought economic gain for the black masses in a separate and racial position of their own, and the black nationalism of Marcus Garvey.

In order to capture this ambivalent estrangement, which conceals the ideological interest (desire to obtain equality of distribution and recognition) of the liberal black bourgeoisie, which has come to be the bearers of ideological domination in "black America," I will apply my structural understanding of consciousness formation to the constitution of Du Bois's own bourgeois consciousness and understanding of consciousness formation, which deconstructs the "doubleness" ideology.

STRUCTURALISM ON DU BOIS'S DOUBLE-CONSCIOUSNESS

Whereas I am suggesting that historically "the revelation of this world," the American (upper-middle class and racist) social structure, forced African consciousness to assume the agential moments of the American world's practical consciousness, for the Du Bois of the *Souls*, which views the constitution of consciousness through both physical and cultural processes as mediated by the bourgeois ideology of nationalism, this "revelation" does not efface the "doubleness" (African and American) of the "souls" or consciousness of black folk; but makes it difficult to reconcile the "two thoughts" in order for them to be in the world. That is, for the Du Bois of *The Souls*, the differentiated and divergent behaviors of the Negro from white America are part of his "innate sense of blackness," or "Negro blood," and the aim of the Negro is "to merge his double self into a better and truer self. In this merging he wishes neither of the older selves to be lost. He would not Africanize America, for America has too much to teach the world and Africa. He would not bleach his Negro soul in a flood of white Americanism, for he knows that Negro blood has a message for the world. He simply wishes to make it possible for a man to be both a Negro and an American, without being cursed and spit upon by his fellows, without having the doors of opportunity closed roughly in his face."

This is Du Boisian double consciousness as a reference to black American biculturalism. It is my position, however, that the construct does not adequately capture the sociohistorical nature of black American consciousness; rather it speaks to Du Bois's ambivalence towards the American nation-state and his purposive-rationale, to recursively organize and reproduce the Protestant ethic of the society in order to obtain equality of opportunity, distribution, and recognition for all black folks amidst racial discrimination. This ambivalent position characterizes many liberal blacks who shared and share Du Bois's social class position.

Hence, Du Bois's construct deconstructed from its racial and national ideology is not really a reference to biculturalism; it instead highlights the aforementioned ambivalence. Let me elaborate. From my understanding of the constitution of black consciousness through disavowal, the former slaves, as interpellated "other" agents of the social structure, at the moment of antagonism in the American world's "ideological apparatuses," construct and constructed their consciousness, like their white counterparts, by warring against the ideals and practices associated with the "other" for the "pure" practical consciousness of authority, not because, as Du Bois points out, they were trying to reconcile these two racial and national "souls" into one distinct consciousness, but in order to be in the socially constructed American capitalist racial world and reject the contempt to which they are subject: "He simply wishes to make it possible for a man to be both a Negro and an American, without being cursed and spit upon by his fellows, without having the doors of opportunity closed roughly in his face." That is, the majority of the slaves attempted to live up to what master signifies as proper human conduct against the un-human-like qualities that is or was master's representation of the former slave as an "other."

This does not mean that the consciousness of the slave, as an African, was or is obliterated, or for that matter is a pathological reaction to whites, as a result of the slavery process (Myrdal, 1944; Liebow, 1967; Berger, 1967), only that the master, through the production and reproduction of the representation of Africanness in and through their ideological apparatuses, used the African's very own initial practical consciousness against them to legitimate the relationship that delimits their "pure" non-African social structure and material practice.

In other words, the African survivals—in courtship practices, dance, familial roles, folktales, language, music, names, proverbs, and religious beliefs and practice (Herskovits, 1941; Karenga, 1993; Holloway, 1990)—initially practiced by the Africans were mirrored back to them as negative ways of Being (ungodly, licentious, emotional, irrational, uncivilized, etc.), which in relation to that of white Americanism (godly, pious, obedient, pure, civilized, rational, diligent, etc.) were un-human-like, and which laws of the American capitalist "ideological mechanical solidarity" prohibited them from practicing.

Du Bois's argument in *The Souls*, by relying on the reference to "Negro blood" as mediated by the concept of nation, is that this relationship gives the "Negroes" an invariant "twoness" for understanding reality: the practical consciousness they begin and began with (in his view their "innate" African spirituality, and "love of harmony and beauty"), as it is or was mirrored back to them from the master, and the "pure" practical consciousness of the master. Thus the "twoness" Du Bois alludes to, in this understanding, is between two opposing ontologies, African and white American, grounded in both cultural processes and physical differences.

My structural reading diametrically opposes this racialized "double" episteme take of Du Bois and many of his later liberal nationalist or culturalist followers (Gilroy, 1993; West, 1993; Allen, 2001) who want to hold on to his concept to explain black identity as somehow distinct from that of the American one because of their "improvisational communalism," "musical and spiritual ideals," or "excitement and emotionalism" as seen by conservatives (Sowell, 1975, 1981; Murray, 1984); instead, I believe that the validity of Du Bois's construct lies in the fact that it highlights the "class racism" of the black identity that for so long served as the bearers of ideological domination for the "race."

In other words, given the declining significance of race and the bourgeois ideology of nationalism (supplanted today by culture) as factors in determining the nature and origin of consciousness, my view is that black consciousness is not singular and homogenized defined by its dualism; instead it is multiple and diverse, differentially related to and dominated by those blacks (upper and middle class blacks) who have internalized the protestant ethic of the American capitalist world as their practical consciousness against all other adaptive responses (i.e., black communism, tribalism, homosexuality, feminism, etc.), which they assessed in terms of the "racial class" basis of the society. It is in reference to their (liberal black bourgeoisie or middle class) being-in-the-world that Du Bois's double consciousness has its validity.

To understand this position better, let us look at it from my structural perspective by applying my theoretical understanding of consciousness formation to the development of Du Bois's own consciousness, and extrapolating his experiences as the historical norm for a particular group of black folks, i.e., the liberal black bourgeoisie, who, like Du Bois, internalized the middle class/racial protestant ideology of the American social structure.

Again my understanding of consciousness formation posits that it is the legal regulations of a society, its "lexicons and representations of signification," its rules of conduct that are sanctioned (as outlined by the power elites) which represents the objective conditions (social structure) of society that structures social relations and constitutes the "ideological" materials by which consciousness is recursively organized and reproduced in material practice as "practical-consciousness."

The general understanding is that individual actors (irreducibly situated subjects) are relationally socialized within society — its semiotic field or predefined and predetermined lexicons and representations of signification, i.e., the field of socialization "and its investment in reproducing and naturalising the structures of power" (Slemon, 1995:47). This socialization takes place through "ideological apparatuses," which in American society represent an ideological flanking for the protestant ethic and the spirit of capitalism, controlled by socialized institutional regulators. The relation between the two runs this way: societal power operates through a complex relationship between ideological apparatuses (i.e., the law, education, rituals, family etc.) and institutional regulators who appropriate and manufacture lexicons and representations of signification of individuals in order to consolidate and legitimate society as a natural "order" and to reproduce individuals as deployable units of that order.

Within the framework of this theoretical model, Du Bois, as an irreducibly situated subject, is an interpellated subject, a constituting unit of the American Protestant "class racial" social structure. Du Bois is socialized through ideological apparatuses, i.e., an Episcopalian family, the Episcopalian church of his youth, at Fisk, Harvard, Berlin, etc., in the society's (reified consciousness) semiotic field established by institutional regulators who, on the one hand, subscribe to an Enlightenment ethos, "enframed" by the purposive-rationality of the Protestant ethic, as mediated by the concept of nation for themselves (insiders); and, on the other hand, structurally prescribe ("other outsiders")an unchanging subhuman condition for Du Bois and people who look like him given their skin color and alleged inferior intellect, justified through that same "racial class" ideological ethos, i.e., whites are rational, civilized, etc., and blacks are sophomoric, emotional, barbarous, etc.

Du Bois's eccentricity as a structurally differentiated, discriminated against black "other outsider" "is his driving ambition to excel intellectually and psychologically to become 'a fellow of Harvard'" (Bell, 1996: 98), and recursively reproduce the "pure" agential moments of his society in spite of the ideas and practices (i.e., segregation, prejudice, etc.) stemming from Harvard and the American world around him, which suggest he cannot on account of his "physical" racial inferiority:

> At Fisk, the problem of race was faced openly and essential racial equality asserted and natural inferiority strenuously denied. In some cases the teachers expressed this theory; in most cases the student opinion naturally forced it. At Harvard, on the other hand, I began to face scientific race dogma: first of all, evolution and the "Survival of the Fittest." It was continually stressed in the community and in classes that there was a vast difference in the development of the whites and the "lower" races; that this could be seen in the physical development of the Negro . . . .
>
> I do not know how I came first to form my theories of race. The process was probably largely unconscious. The differences of personal appearance between me and my fellows, I must have been conscious of when quite young. Whatever distinctions came because of that did not irritate me; they rather exalted me be-

cause, on the whole, while I was still a youth, they gave me exceptional position and a chance to excel rather than handicapping me.

Then of course, when I went South to Fisk, I became a member of a closed racial group with rites and loyalties, with a history and a corporate future, with an art and philosophy. I received these eagerly and expanded them so that when I came to Harvard the theory of race separation was quite in my blood. I did not seek contact with my white fellow students. On the whole I rather avoided them. I took it for granted that we were training ourselves for different careers in worlds largely different. There was not the slightest idea of the permanent subordination and inequality of my world. Nor again was there any idea of racial amalgamation. I resented the assumption that we desired it (Du Bois, 1984 [1940]: 97-101).

In this framework, accordingly, Du Bois is an interpellated discriminated against minority, a member of a structurally differentiated "class-in-itself," blacks, within the American ideological mechanical solidarity, who is attempting to be a "coworker in the kingdom of culture" as defined by the institutional regulators, rich, white, protestant men, of his society. He is prevented from doing so, becoming an institutional regulator in the larger American society, because of race and class prejudice (i.e., structural differentiation), which indexed him with all blacks, the majority of whom, according to Du Bois, were lowly and backward because they were handicapped by race prejudice, ignorance, and dire poverty.

Alienated from both groups, whites because he is black and blacks because he lacks their emotionalism, improvisation, and musical styles, Du Bois seeks, "through the leadership of men like myself" (i.e., his pan-African bourgeois nationalist "Talented Tenth"), to define and apply his own cultural background (New England Way) to his segregated "poor" race or nation in America who do not have a double consciousness, but are characterized, according to Du Bois, by their "Africanism," i.e., emotionalism and spiritualism:

> For this group [(the Negroes or blacks)] I built my plan of study and accomplishment. Through the leadership of men like myself and my fellows, we were going to have these enslaved Israelites out of the still enduring bondage in short order. It was a battle which might conceivably call for force, but I could think of it mainly as a battle of wits; of knowledge and deed, which by sheer reason and desert, must eventually overwhelm the forces of hate, ignorance and reaction (Du Bois, 1968: 112-113).

Thus, the early Du Bois, consciously and unconsciously, accepts the structurally differentiated racial and class understandings of the social structure, and recursively reproduces its "pure" ethics in his praxis through the prisms of his liberal bourgeois black national Protestantism. That is, Du Bois wants to be a fellow at Harvard in order to acquire (through solipsistic hard work) the knowledge, class and status position, which will allow him to be a "coworker in the kingdom of culture" through his deeds based on that knowledge. However, Du Bois is (as a discriminated against minority) also ambivalent about Harvard and the American cultural world because of their racial ideas, which keep the majority of his "group" unequal to whites and enslaved as a structurally differentiated "class-in-itself" known as blacks, who have a distinct consciousness because of their emotionalism and spiritualism stemming from their "black blood." At the moment of antagonism, as an "other," within the American "other world," which is paradoxically also his world, Du Bois shuns it to build a plan of study and accomplishment (pan-African bourgeois nationalism as led by their "Talented Tenth") for "the Negroes," who lack his "otherworldly" class training acquired from Harvard and growing up in Great Barrington.

It is this ambivalence, the desire to "excel" and reject the contempt to which he is subject, Du Bois, using late nineteenth and early twentieth century racial science and ideology, captures with the notion of biculturalism or double consciousness. This reference is merely perspectival and ideological, concealing Du Bois's racial class interest amidst the discriminatory effects of American society: to define and prove black self-worth along the purposive-rationale of obtaining equality of opportunity and recognition in the larger American society. In other words, Du Bois's ambivalence does not bless him with two distinct epistemologies or ontologies, as his double consciousness construct by relying on the racial and national ideology of the late nineteenth and early twentieth century reads.

There are no African structural institutions (Fisk, during Du Bois's stance, was dominated by white teachers—with the exception of one black, William Morris—"from New England or from the New Englandized Middle West")[4] from which Du Bois would have interpretively developed an African ethos. His only understanding of African is revealed to him through the discriminatory identifications of institutional regulators of the "other world" (his world), at Harvard, and the fully visible agential moments of those, i.e., the poor blacks at Fisk, who recursively appear to reproduce the discriminatory identity (i.e., their "emotionalism" and "innate love of harmony and beauty") that delimited the white world his teachers at Fisk were teaching or applying to the Negroes in the South.

Instead, the ambivalence places Du Bois in a "liminal space" wherein alternative meanings and practices from that of his society may arise, given that the ideals of power are revealed to be something that they are not, socially constructed as opposed to natural. In the case of Du Bois, however, the ambivalence produced homogenization or the drive for equality of opportunity, distribution, and recognition, i.e., "to attain self-conscious manhood . . . without being cursed and spit upon by his fellows, without having the doors of Opportunity closed roughly in his face."

In Bhabhaian terms, in other words, the assumption of the "pure" ideals of authority, "class racism," which Du Bois recursively organizes and reproduces as liberal pan-African bourgeois nationalism led by the Talented Tenth of the race constructing a plan of study for blacks "to attain self conscious manhood," i.e., equality of distribution and recognition, along the lines of: "(1) monogamous nuclear family organization; (2) temperance and orderliness as behavioral principles, including thrift and internalization of disciplined work habits; (3) favorable disposition toward formal education and training in the ways of urban civilization; and (4) legitimation of class hierarchy within the racial community" (Reed, 1997: 28). Thus Du Bois does not really seek to define black consciousness, but within this perspective and ideological foundation or purposive-rationale he seeks to institutionalize blacks in the American social formation.

Du Bois's Purposive-rationale

In sum, the institutional regulators (rich, white, Protestant men) of Dr. Du Bois's era subscribe to the ethos of equality among men, exercising their God given inalienable rights to pursue freely economic gain for its own sake in a particular "calling." They maintain and recursively organize these ideas aided by racial slavery and Jim Crow segregation, justifying them by pointing to the inferiority and inhumanity of the non-white Africans, who possess an "identity-in-differential" to the civilized whites because of their emotionalism and innate sense of blackness. These ideas and practices are taught in the home, are codified in the laws, and are subsequently justified by scientific dogma and evidence (Social Darwinism), which is published and taught in schools.

Dr. Du Bois is not exempt from these ideas given his Protestant New England Victorian upbringing and Harvard education, which made him a typical son of the Enlightenment (Black Anglo Saxon Protestant) like his white counterparts, "who viewed society [(and the world at-large)] largely through the prism of [(Protestant)] ethics and spirituality" (Marable, 1986: 51). What differentiates Du Bois from his white counterparts, however, is his black skin, which did not prevent him from becoming an institutional regulator, i.e., he was an Atlanta University professor and longtime editor of the NAACP's *Crisis*, but (from the position of the white power elites) this indexed him with all blacks as a subordinate racial class-in-itself.

It should be mentioned, that Du Bois as a structurally differentiated discriminated against "other," does not, given his phenomenological meditation, initially come up with a different "form of orientation in the world"; again, he is an "other" because of race and class prejudice or structural differentiation, which prevents him from living as an institutional regulator within the larger society. Du Bois, in practically every respect, subscribes to the understanding of the "other world," but wants their substantive values—"for the words I longed for, and all their dazzling opportunities, were theirs, not mine. But they should not keep these prizes, I said; some, all, I would wrest from them"—for his kind, i.e., black folk, who were poor not because of the "innateness" of the negative stereotypes revealed by the "other world," which for Du Bois they (not him) clearly demonstrated, but because they were unfortunate, which Du Bois, as an agent of the Protestant ethic believed, "could easily be mended by thrift and sacrifice," "knowledge," and "accomplishment."

This is the estrangement, outside of the racial and national ideology of the 19th century, explicitly embedded in the construct, that gives rise to Dr. Du Bois's (as a paragon for his class, i.e., the black bourgeoisie) "double consciousness" construct, and makes it distinct, for example, from Antonio Gramsci's "two theoretical consciousnesses." Du Bois's ideology and experience is rooted in the structure of meaning and reference that is the semiotic field of his society. That is, Du Bois's initial agency, and hence his ambivalence, results from structural contradictions. Du Bois's subjective position is a result of the power and resistance of one hegemonic historical bloc, which he initially opposes "by convicting it [(the ideals of upper-middle class Americanism) of nonidentity with itself" (Adorno, 1973 [1966]: 147), not by positing a differing ontology or epistemology.

Gramsci's "two theoretical consciousnesses," on the contrary, imply that the social actor is divided between two hegemonic articulatory principles, one practical and the other ideal with its own articulatory principles. Du Bois's ideals and practices, which stem from the articulatory principles of one historical bloc, are one and the same, which, under the purview of late nineteenth and early twentieth century social thought that prevented racial integration, became for Du Bois liberal pan-African bourgeois nationalism as led by the "Talented Tenth" of the black race seeking equality of opportunity, distribution, and recognition for black folk in order to reject the contempt to which they were subject.

Du Bois is not seeking to institute into the American social world an alternative consciousness, or non-identity that opposes his Protestant ethic and the spirit of capitalism. Instead, Du Bois responds to the paradox of being ideologically a bourgeois middle class American (although he understood most of the ideas to be universal), with no other ideals/practices to exercise in the world, and yet his existence is negated by the rationale of this same ideology by convicting the American social structure of nonidentity with itself. (As Du Bois tells us, "I was blithely European and imperialist in outlook; democratic as democracy was conceived in America" (Du Bois, 1984 [1968]: 32). Du Bois chose to address the institutional regulators of the American mechanical solidarity, given their negative representation of him and people who looked like him, because they subordinated "the will and well being of blacks individually and collectively to those of the dominant group" (Bell, 1996: 92). He wanted democracy and economic gain for his people.[5] His aim was, since "there is substantial agreement in laws, language and religion . . . there is a satisfactory adjustment of economic life . . . " (Du Bois, 1971 [1897]: 182), for the men of the two races to strive together for their "race ideals" rather "than in isolation," which the racist signifiers of the society attempted to prevent for the majority of blacks, who remained a class-in-itself, not because they had an identity-in-differential to that of whites, but due to structural differentiation, i.e., Jim Crow laws and worldwide racial prejudice backed by "scientific evidence":

> The absolute equality of races—physical, political and social—is the founding stone of world peace and human advancement. No one denies great differences of gift, capacity and attainment among individuals of all races, but the voice of science, religion and practical politics is one in denying the God-appointed existence of super-races, or of races naturally and inevitably and eternally inferior.
> That in the vast range of time, one group should in its industrial technique, or social organization, or spiritual vision, lag a few hundred years behind another, or forge fitfully ahead, or come to differ decidedly in thought, deed and ideal, is proof of the essential richness and variety of human nature, rather than proof of the co-existence of demi-gods and apes in human form. The doctrine of racial equality does not interfere with individual liberty, rather, it fulfils it. And of all the various criteria by which masses of men have in the past been prejudged and classified, that of the color of the skin and texture of the hair, is surely the most adventitious and idiotic (Du Bois, 1997 [1921]: 41).

Du Bois, as this passage highlights, wants the "ideological universals," i.e., sovereignty, equality, justice, the democratic and economic ideals etc., of his society for his race, which he sees (as "lowly," "backward," "ignorant and poor," etc., not because of their innate characteristics but as a result of social discrimination) through the light of his recursively organized and reproduced protestant bourgeois ideology. He wants equality of opportunity, recognition and distribution for his race, "the backward and suppressed groups of mankind," which will be achieved, once discrimination is abandoned, through self-control, self knowledge, intelligence, and the help of their intelligentsia:

> It is the duty of the world to assist in every way the advance of the backward and suppressed groups of mankind. The rise of all men is a menace to no one and is the highest human ideal; it is not an altruistic benevolence, but the one road to world salvation.
>
> For the purpose of raising such peoples to intelligence, self-knowledge and self-control, their intelligentsia of right ought to be recognized as the natural leaders of their groups.
>
> The insidious and dishonorable propaganda, which, for selfish ends, so distorts and denies facts as to represent the advancement and development of certain races of men as impossible and undesirable, should be met with widespread dissemination of the truth. The experiment of making the Negro slave a free citizen in the United States is not a failure; the attempts at autonomous government in Haiti and Liberia are not proofs of the impossibility of self-government among black men; the experience of Spanish America does not prove that mulatto democracy will not eventually succeed there; the aspirations of Egypt and India are not successfully to be met by sneers at the capacity of darker races.
>
> We who resent the attempt to treat civilized men as uncivilized, and who bring in our hearts grievance upon grievance against those who lynch the untried, disfranchise the intelligent, deny self-government to educated men, and insult the helpless, we complain; but not simply or primarily for ourselves—more especially for the millions of our fellows, blood of our blood, and flesh of our flesh, who have not even what we have—the power to complain against monstrous wrong, the power to see and to know the source of our oppression (Du Bois, 1997 [1921]: 41-42).

The "double consciousness," then, deconstructed from its racial ideology as mediated by the concept of nation is not the sign of the distinctiveness of "Negro" culture and character; rather it is the ambivalence Du Bois (whose life represents a paragon of black bourgeois life) feels being ideologically American (upper middle class) yet being denied the fruits of this ideal in material practice because of the lowly representation of his "racial class" status, which he must war against to prove his humanity by recursively organizing and reproducing the structural "pure" terms of authority. In short, the construct is the embodiment of Du Bois's "class racism" as a black Protestant liberal nationalist, Du Bois desires for his race and nation the bourgeois ideals of the "spirit of capitalism" in order to reject the contempt to which blacks as second class citizens are subject. He advocates, in the face of racial discrimination, for the "educated" elites ("The Talented Tenth") of the black nation ("pan-Africanism") throughout the world to establish "Negro" institutions "for the purpose of raising such peoples to intelligence, self-knowledge and self-control." Du Bois makes this ambivalence clear when he writes at the tender age of ninety: "that dichotomy which all my life has characterized my thought: how far can love for my oppressed race accord with love for the oppressing country? And when these loyalties diverge, where shall my soul find refuge" (Du Bois, 1986[1968]: 169).

Consequently, it was the despair of being in this unremitting "ambivalent space"—"[t]he colored people of America are coming to face the fact quite calmly that most white Americans do not like them, and are planning neither for their survival, nor for their definite future if it involves free, self assertive modern manhood" (Du Bois, 1971 [1935]: 401)—, and Du Bois's continual "phenomenological meditation" on his social situation that leads him, in his controversial article "A Negro Nation Within the Nation" published in June 1935, to reject the sedimented and codified structures of signification of his world, for another form of orientation in the world, i.e., black communism led by its "Talented tenth," which in the order of early twentieth-century anticommunist social life made him an "other" again.[6] The rest of black America, Du Bois, in his last autobiography, written in exile in Ghana, argues, have chosen to "follow [(as agents of the Protestant ethic, and its practice the spirit of capitalism)] in the footsteps of western acquisitive society, with its exploitation of labor, its monopoly of land and resources, and with private profit for the smart and unscrupulous in a world of poverty, disease, and ignorance, as the natural end of human culture." This predatory and soul-less end he argued, the black people of the world, as a collective led by "the advanced [(i.e., predestined)] guard of Negro people" (i.e., black people in America), should have avoided:

> Refuse to be cajoled or to change your way of life so as to make a few of your fellows rich at the expense of a mass of workers growing poor and sick, and remaining without schools so that a few black men can have automobiles.
>
> Africa here is a real danger which you must avoid or return to the slavery from which you are emerging.[7]

NOTES

1. The ideological totality defined here parallels Gramsci's ideological "historical bloc." See Ernesto Laclau and Chantal Mouffe's *Hegemony and Socialist Strategy: Towards a Radical Democratic Politics* (1985) pp. 67.

2. My position, unlike postmodernist theorists of the likes of Dorothy Smith, Homi K. Bhabha, or Chantal Mouffe, is that marginality (regardless if the subject is conceived, "as the articulation of an ensemble of subject positions"), unless the marginalized group repudiates and attempts to reconstitute society by formulating a new

social structure, does not and can not lead to diversity within the social structure in which marginalization takes place. In fact, the sense of diversity prescribed by these theorists is a sense of false consciousness based on the focus on the body in theory construction, which the postmodern turn proffers. Du Bois, for example, toward the end of his life, becomes a heterogeneous subject by rejecting the American social structure for another form of being in the world, i.e., a black nationalist communist, which he sought to institutionalize.

3. As Francis L. Broderick (1959: 3) points out, Du Bois in his early years "learned the capitalist ethic of late nineteenth-century America: 'Wealth was the result of work and saving and the rich rightly inherited the earth. The poor, on the whole, were to be blamed. They were lazy or unfortunate, and if unfortunate their fortunes could easily be mended by thrift and sacrifice.'" Thus, in his Being-in-the-world, Du Bois, given his lack of encounter with overt discrimination (with the exception of a few racial encounters with the Irish, who were looked down upon by everyone in his community because they were poor) understands the world and the people in it through the dissolution and reformulation of his Protestant Americanism in material practice. It is in terms of this structural consciousness that he understands the racial "otherness" of the "Negroes" in the South, who, I am arguing, exercise a form of Americanism hampered by the "unfortunates" of racial discrimination. Du Bois, on the contrary, early on in his life sees their "otherness" as being part and parcel of or an aspect of their Africanness, i.e., their "doubleness," an understanding, as Adolph Reed argues he never goes back to given his later Marxist ideological leanings.

4. Du Bois, W.E.B. (1986 [1968]. *The Autobiography of W.E.B. Du Bois: A Soliloquy on Viewing My Life from the Last Decade of its First Century*. New York: International Publishers, Pp. 108.

5. Du Bois's liberal political orientation is at the center of his strife with the conservative black nineteenth-century leader, Booker T. Washington.

6. The locus of causality for Du Bois's push for communism I am not arguing is a result of the contradictory practices of his society or the system. On the contrary, my argument is that Du Bois's decision is a result of his phenomenological meditation on the nature of things. For it is feasible to have contradictory practices and yet continue the practices that give rise to the contradiction.

7. Du Bois quoted in, Hunton, Alphaeus W. (1970). "W.E.B. Du Bois: the meaning of his life," Pp. 131-137. In *Black Titan: W.E.B. Du Bois*, Edited by John Henrik Clarke et al. Boston: Beacon Press.

Chapter Four

Black Consciousness Today

In the course of this work I have attempted to examine the nature of black practical consciousness and its relation to Du Bois's double consciousness construct. The underlying assumption has been that the construct black double consciousness should be understood in relation to the purposive rationality (i.e., the imaginary "fictive ethnicity," or "class racism," (Etienne Balibar's terms)) of the liberal black (male) bourgeoisie, which, following the civil war, wanted equality of opportunity, distribution, and recognition with its white counterpart, rather than a real community, or nation, defined by its "doubleness" or dual ethnicity.

An important starting point was to trace the history of black America in slavery. Slavery had a profound impact on the political, social, and economic life of the African slaves who came in the main from West Africa where diverse cultural practices existed. While scholars of the pathological-pathogenic school have viewed the impact of slavery on these differences as obstacles to the development of an authentic black culture or social cohesion, scholars of the adaptive-vitality school have pointed to the retentions of Africanisms in ways of thinking, behaving, and speaking.

Subsuming the black American historical experience within a structurationist understanding of consciousness formation, I rejected the position of both schools. I demonstrated instead that black practical consciousness is multiple and diverse, but dominated by the practical consciousness of the liberal black (male) bourgeoisie or middle class which for a long time served as the bearers of ideological domination in American society.

Specifically, I reinterpreted the historiography of how the institution of slavery impacted and re-shaped African practical consciousnesses. Africans were introduced into the American Protestant capitalist social structure as slaves. American whites represented their African practical consciousnesses as primitive forms of being-in-the-world to that of the dominant American white Protestant bourgeois social order (Patterson, 1982: 38).

From this relational perspective, and in keeping with the dominant structural interpretation of the pathological-pathogenic school, I illustrated the structural forces—race, class, and status—that eventually, under the "contradictory principles of marginality and integration" (Patterson, 1982: 46), shaped the majority of African consciousness as a "racial class-in-itself" (blacks), a "caste in class," forced to embody the structural terms (bourgeois ideals in the guise of the protestant ethic) of the dominant American (capitalist) social relations of production, over all other "alternative" African adaptive responses to its then organizational form, slavery. This embodiment of bourgeois ideals, in the guise of the protestant ethic, by the majority of Africans amidst their poor material conditions, I conclude, eventually made the struggle for freedom amongst a few blacks nothing more than a black middle class phenomenon as the more "liberal" arm of the best of the house servants, artisans, and free blacks from the North, acting as a structurally differentiated "racial class-for-itself," a "caste in class," sought to define the black situation for all blacks, in terms of the society's bourgeois ideals (temperance, economic gain for its own sake, and good moral character), which they acquired through "ideological apparatuses" defined by their white Protestant capitalist masters who viewed black emotionalism, intuition, disobedience, "immorality," and "barbarity" as contrary to white civilized Protestantism. It is, I argue, the ambivalence of the liberal black (male) bourgeoisie or middle class, their *desire* to obtain equality of distribution and recognition amidst their *derision* and contempt for the racial discrimination they face, in the American social structure that W.E.B. Du Bois (as a member of this class) captures with his double consciousness construct.

Thus, as I demonstrate in chapter three, through an analysis of W.E.B. Du Bois's *habitus* or "practical consciousness," the embodiment of middle class interest, the agential moments of the American social structure, amidst the racial discrimination faced by blacks as they sought and seek to exercise these interests in order to better their material conditions and obtain equality of distribution and recognition, is the sole reason for this double consciousness or biculturation highlighted by Du Bois.

This conclusion negates the adaptive-vitality school's attempt to validate externally black American consciousness as dual or bicultural. Although Du Bois's double consciousness construct may have started off as the notion that black consciousness is divided between two distinct epistemologies and ontologies, given his reliance on nineteenth century racial and national ideology to understand black "practical consciousness" amidst that of white protestant

America, my sociohistorical understanding and deconstruction of the construct reveals it to be more of a description of ambivalence, amongst the liberal black bourgeoisie or middle and upper middle class blacks, rather than a distinct ethos from that of the protestant ethic by which many black Americans (with bourgeois upper middle class sensibilities) recursively organize and reproduce their material resource framework.

In short, I conclude that the construct is the embodiment of Du Bois's, as a representative of the liberal black bourgeoisie, "class racism;" Du Bois, through the prism of liberal black Protestant nationalism, desires for his predominantly "poor" race and nation the bourgeois ideals of the American capitalist social structure in order to reject the contempt to which blacks as second class citizens are subject. He advocates, in the face of class and racial discrimination, for the "educated" elites ("The Talented Tenth") of the black nation ("pan-Africanism") throughout the world to establish "Negro" institutions "for the purpose of raising such peoples to intelligence, self-knowledge and self-control" so that they can be recognized in the kingdom of cultures, i.e., obtain equality of opportunity, distribution, and recognition with their white counterparts. Du Bois, after 1903, I conclude, dismissed this liberal ideological and practical orientation for black national communism, which denounced the class basis and social structure of inequality in American society.

THE CONTEMPORARY BLACK AMERICAN

Black Americans today under consumer capitalism have gone a long way from living up to the image of their puritan masters—thrift, frugality, and relentless self-denial can hardly be considered at the present time to be their outstanding characteristics. Yet the essence of "the spirit of racial capitalism" and the ambivalence, which characterized the early Du Bois's own consciousness are still the basis for their practical consciousness under late twentieth and early twenty-first century post-industrial (consumerist) capitalist organization.

Led by a segment of their population, the liberal black bourgeoisie—who's adaptive-vitality to enslavement was incorporation of the structural terms, i.e., class and status, of the American social structure—with a middle class sensibility and concerned with civil rights, assimilation, and "positive" black images, i.e., agents of the protestant ethic, their continual gaze "back upon the eye of power" to allow them to partake in the order of things, comes from, and is driven by, their reproduction of the reified consciousness of the rational American capitalist state. The state through ideological apparatuses, i.e., the law, public education, churches, the organization of the family, interpellates and "embourgeois" these black subjects with their wants, needs, and ideals (consciousness), which they subscribe to and ideologically reproduce in their own Negro Academies, i.e., black colleges, churches, fraternities and sororities, etc, in order "to attain self conscious manhood" and reject the contempt to which they are subject.

The struggle of this segment of black America, prior to (when they numbered 5 percent of the black population), and since (25 percent), Du Bois, has been for equality of opportunity (for distribution and recognition), because that is what has been lacking in their relation with whites, not to recognize or exercise a distinct ethos, which never materialized amongst the majority of the masses given that power delimited the social structure they had to be in by marginalizing ("class racism") their very being, i.e., African ethos, in relation to white bourgeois Protestantism. This is the relational structure all Africans interpellated in the American social structure, warred against (the marginalization of their being as an "other") in order "to be" in the American social structure of capitalist inequality. They did so, that is, the African, a deployable unit of the American social structure, sought to be an agent of the social structure by having to disprove, warred against through the exercise of the praxis of the social structure, like their white counterparts, the ideas of the "other" by which they were marginalized.

Amongst the liberal black bourgeoisie, however, the end product was a "colored" American, no hybrid in the Bhabhaian sense, whose only subversive act, given the need to disprove the contempt to which they are subject, is to recursively organize and reproduce the "pure" identity of authority to its "purest form" in order to obtain equality of opportunity, distribution, recognition with their white counterparts (Frazier, 1957; Hare, 1965 [1991]; Woodson, 1933 [1969]).[1]

During the Black power era (1965-1979) there was an attempt to turn the gaze inward and establish Negro academies that grappled with the needs of a people as opposed to reproducing in their material practices a soulless (ideological-mechanical) reified-consciousness presented as the nature of life as such (the middle class response). This, however, came to pass as J. Edgar Hoover and his "counterintelligence program" sought to "expose, disrupt, misdirect, discredit, or otherwise neutralize the activities of black nationalist, hate-type organizations and groups, their leadership, spokesmen, membership, and supporters, and to counter their propensity for violence and civil disorder" (Hoover, 1997 [1967]: 134).

What was produced in turn was the continual disjuncture between the ideologies of those looking to turn the gaze inward (i.e., black nationalist, conservatives, pan Africanist, communist groups, and religious groups such as the Nation of Islam) and those gazing back upon the eye of power (i.e., the liberal black bourgeoisie) for recognition. The latter, as was the case during slavery, prevailed, and their continual protest for economic gain and recognition is rationalized and represented in the reified consciousness of the society as the proper way of doing things, which in turn is taught in the society's "ideological apparatuses" using representatives who have succeeded (black bourgeoisie) that way as examples for the rest of the discriminated against (black underclass, pan-Africanists, nationalists, homosexuals, communists, etc.). This integrationist aim for all of black America is the drive behind Tavis Smiley's new work, *The Covenant with Black America* (2006), which seeks to lay a liberal black middle class plan of action for black America to integrate more into the fabric of American capitalism amidst the continual contempt to which they are subject as a result of the ever-increasing proletarianization and criminalization of the black masses.

Thus, contemporarily, the historical evolution of the practices of this group of blacks, who have led the integrationist movement, has resulted in the legitimation of the Protestant and capitalist practices of the American social structure as the nature of reality and existence as such, and the nature (i.e., structural terms—class and status) by which all (blacks) must assess their being-in-the-world.

This acceptance of the structural (class) terms of the society has led to the "declining significance of race" as black participation in the social structure has resulted in their continual class stratification in which a dwindling middle class living in suburbs is assimilated and isolated from an "underclass," living in urban inner-cities, who do not have a distinct practical consciousness from that of the black middle class as suggested by conservative integrationists such as Thomas Sowell (1975, 1981) and Shelby Steele (1990); on the contrary, their conspicuous consumptive practices in post-industrial capitalist America are a pathological-pathogenic reflection of the structural terms of the society constrained by the poor material conditions of their structured resource framework (Gutiérrez, 2004; Geronimus and Thompson, 2004; Mocombe, 2004).

In other words, the black underclass, structurally differentiated permanent "others" i.e., discriminated against minority, due to low level of education and few marketable skills, they, black underclass, are segregated from a scattered black bourgeoisie who ape after the American dream. Isolated from both white and black middle class America, they (i.e., the black underclass) are an entrapped population of poor persons, used, unwanted, and unemployed, welfare dependents who, given their ideological indoctrination by institutional regulators of the media, schools, and other ideological apparatuses, also ape after the American dream (Wilson, 1978; 1981; Massey and Denton, 1993). Subsequently, lately that is, they have developed a commodified way of life among themselves (hip-hop culture) centered on the means that are most likely to provide recognition and "economic gain" i.e., music, athletics, drugs, prostitution, pimping etc., amidst their "hardship in poverty," "poor land and low wages," "race prejudice and legal bonds," and "ignorance and dire poverty."

This commodified way of life in post-industrial capitalist America has become the global youth culture of the twenty-first century. It (hip-hop culture) is a distinctively American cultural phenomenon, which stems from the segregating and differentiating class processes of "the spirit of capitalism." Many black power elites (bourgeois) who have led and continue to lead the integration movement (gazing back to power for recognition) either attempt to clean up elements of "Hip-Hop culture," as a distinct black culture rooted in African spiritual and musical ideals, in order to market and profit from it (Russell Simmons, etc.); or they (Jesse Jackson, Al Sharpton, Bill Cosby, Winston Marsalis, Glenn Loury, Shelbe Steele, Stanley Crouch, members of the Congressional Black Caucus, etc.) shun it, through either a conservative or liberal prism of a Protestant and moralizing ethos, hypocritically disapproving of its promiscuous, nihilistic, masochistic, and homophobic language and form of being in the world—in most cases in favor of Jazz and a moral ethic grounded in the Protestantism of Du Bois's era—which some argue can be transformed either through structural forces (i.e., Affirmative Action and the welfare state) or a form of behaviorism that emphasizes self-love, (nuclear) patriarchal family, education, professional calling, and community, i.e., an "embeddedness" of the Protestant ethic and the spirit of capitalism. In either case, the liberal model which emphasizes structural solutions or the conservative model which emphasize self-help, my point is that this is no ground to argue for a double consciousness; it simply points to the continual struggle of how best to (re) present the racial images of the black, dark-skinned, American—whites seem to prefer the black professional class—within the agential moments (structural variables, i.e., class and status) of racial class gendered Protestantism and its differentiating structural practice, the spirit of capitalism: the black underclass or the professional class.

This contemporary "racial class" ambivalent struggle amongst post-segregationist black American scholars and professionals I see as the parallel to W.E.B. Du Bois's own early ambivalent struggle to disassociate himself from negative images, due to "hardship in poverty," "poor land and low wages," "race prejudice and legal bonds," and "ignorance and dire poverty," in order to partake in the "class" fabric of American sociopolitical life.

In fact, it is the basis for the insistent clamor for this notion of a black double consciousness today (albeit race and nation are now supplanted by African cultural elements) as each generation of blacks strives to partake in the order of things, while attempting to avoid failing and being stigmatized with the entrapped sector of the population who looks like them, and who paradoxically fail because of the Protestant capitalist social structure by which they reproduce their lives (Watkins, 1998; Mason, 1996; Reed, 1997).

This reading is not intended to discredit the dynamics involved in blacks trying to establish a distinct ethos; but to suggest that this takes place within a singular ideological mechanical solidarity, a reified consciousness, dominated by the black middle class and "underclass" agents of the protestant ethic, who position themselves as the bearers of ideological domination for black folk and bar those (Nation of Islam, black communists, feminists, homosexuals, etc.) who misinterpret their signifiers or choose another form of being-in-the-world from partaking in the order of things.[2]

Paradoxically, given the fact that the latter group (black underclass) is segregated and entrapped, one would think, in light of their poor material conditions, that it is among them that a distinct anti-structural black ethos should have developed, but in fact they identify with the ethos of the larger society—through the black middle class and whites who direct the churches and educational ideological apparatuses in their segregated communities as pastors, principals, and teachers—and ape for American materialism "by any means necessary," i.e., sports, music, drugs, crime, etc. A striving driven by the soulless aim of American Protestant capitalism, which they (black underclass) so desperately attempt to recursively reproduce in their poor material conditions, "to make a few...fellows rich at the expense of a mass of workers growing poor and sick, and remaining without schools so that a few [(predestined)] black men can have automobiles" (Du Bois, 1970).[3]

This is the soul-less, immoral, aim that black practical consciousness has taken after almost 400 years in a soul-less social structure of inequality that seeks to hegemonically dominate the world, exhaust its natural resources, and destroy the environment and humanity. Ideologically concealed under the veneers of a religious Protestantism taught in many mega-churches, many black folks' Protestant Ethic and the spirit of capitalism does not allow them to question or protest against the predatory effects of global capitalism, which is enslaving the world's people of color for the economic gains of the middle class and their slavemasters, the upper-class of owners and high-level executives.

Instead, "the blessings of riches," as a sign of their salvation, is preached every Sunday, and their lives become centered on the accumulation of goods and capital for economic gain and conspicuous consumption. This in spite of the fact that the rise of the black bourgeois middle class, like their white counterparts, is, ironically, at the expense of the world's people of color. Instead of refusing to be cajoled to participate in a world which seeks to make a few of their fellows rich at the expense of the mass of workers of the world growing poor and sick, and remaining without schools, many black folks, like their white counterparts, recursively organize and reproduce their "soul-less" Protestant ethic and the spirit of capitalism so that a few black men can have "bling" "bling" as a sign of their salvation and predestination in the face of poverty related deaths throughout the world and urban America.

How can black folk truly serve as the "moral consciousness" of America amidst the pervasiveness of black on black crime, and the preaching of a Protestant Ethic contingent upon material wealth for a few as a sign of their blessing and salvation? To truly be associated with the righteous nations of the 25th chapter of Matthew in the Holy Bible, and be the moral consciousness of the American nation, the souls' of black folk must be constituted and recognized not by the recognition of its "African-Americanness," but by its worldly attempt to feed the hungry, give drink to the thirsty, shelter the stranger, clothe the naked, visit the sick, and come to the aid of those in prison in a soul-less society that creates the converse of these practices for the sole purpose of proving its predestination via economic gain and military might at the expense of the masses of black America and the world growing poor and sick.

NOTES

1. Even if one were to make the argument, as I take Bhabha to be doing, that hybridity is a necessary result of the interaction between power and the discriminated against; it does not hold that hybridity exists as a subversive force if the discriminated against accepts the terms of those who discriminate against them, which is my argument. Bhabha's emphasis focuses too much on the physical body, devoid of distinct practices, as the site for subversion.

2. There are many blacks in academia who have rejected the normative order of things for an afrocentric worldview and communism. However, being in academia, they have been relegated to an interpretive community, which says and understands the world one way, but lives in it by recursively organizing and reproducing the agential moments of the American Protestant capitalist social structure.

3. Du Bois quoted in, Hunton, Alphaeus w. (1970). "W.E.B. Du Bois: the meaning of his life," Pp. 131-137. In *Black Titan: W.E.B. Du Bois*, Edited by John Henrik Clarke et al. Boston: Beacon Press.

References Cited

Adorno, Theodor W. (2000). *Negative Dialectics*. New York: Continuum.
Allen, Ernest Jr. (2002). "Du Boisian Double Consciousness: The Unsustainable Argument." *The Massachusetts Review*, 43 (2): 217-253.
Allen, Ernest Jr. (1992). "Ever Feeling One's Twoness: 'Double Ideals and 'Double Consciousness' in the Souls of Black Folk." *Critique of Anthropology*, 12 (3): 261-275.
Allen, Richard L. (2001). *The Concept of Self: A Study of Black Identity and Self Esteem*. Detroit: Wayne State University Press.
Althusser, Louis (2001). *Lenin and Philosophy and Other Essays*. New York: Monthly Review Press.
Althusser, Louis and Étienne Balibar (1970). *Reading Capital* (Ben Brewster, Trans.). London: NLB.
Altschuler, Richard (ed.) (1998). *The living Legacy of Marx, Durkheim, and Weber: Applications and Analyses of Classical Sociological Theory by Modern Social Scientists*. New York: Gordian Knot Books.
Appiah, Anthony (1985). "The Uncompleted Argument: Du Bois and the Illusion of Race." *Critical Inquiry*, 12: 21-37.
Aptheker, Herbert (ed.) (1985). *W.E.B. Du Bois Against Racism: Unpublished Essays, Papers, Addresses, 1887-1961*. Amherst: The University of Massachusetts Press.
Archer, Margaret S. (1985). "Structuration versus Morphogenesis." In H.J. Helle and S.N. Eisenstadt (Eds.), *Macro-Sociological Theory: Perspectives on Sociological Theory* (Volume 1) (pp. 58-88). United Kingdom: J.W. Arrowsmith Ltd.
Asante, Molefi Kete (1988). *Afrocentricity*. New Jersey: Africa World.
Asante, Molefi K. (1990a). *Kemet, Afrocentricity and Knowledge*. New Jersey: Africa World.
Asante, Molefi K. (1990b). "African Elements in African-American English." In Joseph E. Holloway (Ed.), *Africanisms in American Culture* (pp. 19-33). Bloomington and Indianapolis: Indiana University Press.

Austin, J.L. (1997). *How to do Things With Words* (Second edition, J.O. Urmson and Marina Sbisà, editors). Cambridge, Massachusetts: Harvard University Press.

Baker, Houston A., Jr. (1985). "The Black Man of Culture: W.E.B. Du Bois and The Souls of Black Folk." In William L. Andrews (Ed.), *Critical Essays on W.E.B. Du Bois* (pp.129-139). Boston: G.K. Hall & Co.

Balibar, Etienne & Immanuel Wallerstein (1991 [1988]). *Race, Nation, Class: Ambiguous Identities*. London: Verso.

Ballantine, Jeanne, H. (1993). *The Sociology of Education: A systematic Analysis* (3rd Edition). New Jersey: Prentice Hall.

Ball, Howard (2000). *The Bakke Case: Race, Education, and Affirmative Action*. Kansas: University Press of Kansas.

Barthes, Roland (1972). *Mythologies* (Annette Lavers, Trans.). New York: Hill and Wang.

Bell, Daniel (1985). *The Social Sciences Since the Second World War*. New Brunswick (USA): Transaction Books.

Bell, Bernard W. et al (editors) (1996). *W. E. B. Du Bois on Race and Culture: Philosophy, Politics, and Poetics*. New York and London: Routledge.

Bell, Bernard W. (1996). "Genealogical Shifts in Du Bois's Discourse on Double Consciousness as the Sign of African American Difference." In Bernard W. Bell et al (Eds.), *W.E.B. Du Bois on Race and Culture: Philosophy, Politics, and Poetics* (pp. 87-108). New York and London: Routledge.

Bell, Bernard W. (1985). "W.E.B. Du Bois's Struggle to Reconcile Folk and High Art." In William L. Andrews (Ed.), *Critical Essays on W.E.B. Du Bois* (pp.106-122). Andrews. Boston: G.K. Hall & Co.

Bennett, Lerone (1982). *Before the Mayflower*. Chicago: Johnson Publishing Company.

Bhabha, Homi (1995a). "Cultural Diversity and Cultural Differences." In Bill Ashcroft et al (Eds.), *The Post-colonial Studies Reader* (pp. 206-209). London and New York: Routledge.

Bhabha, Homi (1995b). "Signs Taken for Wonders." In Bill Ashcroft et al (Eds.), *The Post-colonial Studies Reader* (pp. 29-35). London and New York: Routledge.

Bhabha, Homi (1994). "Remembering Fanon: Self, Psyche and the Colonial Condition." In Patrick Williams and Laura Chrisman (Eds.), *Colonial Discourse and Post-Colonial Theory A Reader* (pp. 112-123). New York: Columbia University Press.

Billingsley, Andrew (1968). *Black Families in White America*. New Jersey: Prentice Hall.

Billingsley, Andrew (1970). "Black Families and White Social Science." *Journal of Social Issues*, 26, 127-142.

Billingsley, Andrew (1993). *Climbing Jacob's Ladder: The Enduring Legacy of African American Families*. New York: Simon & Schuster.

Bizzell, Patricia and Bruce Herzberg (2001). *The Rhetorical Tradition: Readings from Classical Times to the Present*. Boston: Bedford/St. Martin's.

Blassingame, John W. (1972). *The Slave Community: Plantation Life in the Antebellum South*. New York: Oxford University Press.

Boskin, Joseph (1965). "Race Relations in Seventeenth-Century America: The Problem of the Origins of Negro Slavery." In Donald Noel (Ed.), *The Origins of American Slavery and Racism* (pp. 95-105). Ohio: Charles E. Merrill Publishing Co.

Boswell, Terry (1989). "Colonial Empires and the Capitalist World-Economy: A Time Series Analysis of Colonization, 1640-1960." *American Sociological Review*, 54, 180-196.

Bourdieu, Pierre (1990). *The Logic of Practice* (Richard Nice, Trans.). Stanford, California: Stanford University Press.

Bourdieu, Pierre (1984). *Distinction: A Social Critique of the Judgement of Taste* (Richard Nice, Trans.). Cambridge MA: Harvard University Press.

Boxill, Bernard R. (1996). "Du Bois on Cultural Pluralism." In Bell W. Bernard et al (Eds.), *W.E.B. Du Bois on Race and Culture: Philosophy, Politics, and Poetics* (pp. 57-86). New York and London: Routledge.

Brecher, Jeremy and Tim Costello (1998). *Global Village or Global Pillage: Economic Reconstruction from the bottom up* (second ed.). Cambridge, Mass.: South End Press.

Brennan, Teresa (1997). "The Two Forms of Consciousness." *Theory Culture & Society*, 14 (4): 89-96.

Broderick, Francis L. (1959). *W.E.B. Du Bois, Negro Leader in a Time of Crisis*. Stanford, California: Stanford University Press.

Bruce, Dickinson D., Jr. (1992). "W.E.B. Du Bois and the Idea of Double Consciousness." *American Literature*, 64: 299-309.

Caws, Peter (1997). *Structuralism: A Philosophy for the Human Sciences*. New York: Humanity Books.

Chase-Dunn, Christopher and Peter Grimes (1995). "World-Systems Analysis." *Annual Review of Sociology*, 21, 387-417.

Chase-Dunn, Christopher and Richard Rubinson (1977). "Toward a Structural Perspective on the World-System." *Politics & Society*, 7: 4, 453-476.

Chase-Dunn, Christopher (1975). "The effects of international economic dependence on development and inequality: A cross-national study." *American Sociological Review*, 40, 720-738.

Clark, Robert P. (1997). *The Global Imperative: An Interpretive History of the Spread of Humankind*. Boulder, Colorado: Westview Press.

Clarke, John Henrik, et. al. (eds.) (1970). *Black Titan: W.E.B. Du Bois*. Boston: Beacon Press.

Cohen, J. (2002). *Protestantism and Capitalism: The Mechanisms of Influence*. New York: Aldine de Gruyter.

Collinson, Diane (1987). *Fifty Major Philosophers: A Reference Guide*. London: Routledge.

Coser, Lewis (1956). *The functions of social conflict*. New York: The Free Press.

Covino, William A. and David A. Jolliffe (1995). *Rhetoric: concepts, definitions, boundaries*. Needham Heights, Massachusetts: Allyn and Bacon.

Crothers, Charles (2003). "Technical Advances in General Sociological Theory: The Potential Contribution of Post-Structurationist Sociology." *Perspectives*, 26: 3, 3-6.

Crouch, Stanley (1993). "Who are We? Where Did We Come From? Where Are We Going?" In Gerald Early (Ed.), *Lure and Loathing: Essays on Race, Identity, and the Ambivalence of Assimilation* (pp. 80-94). New York: The Penguin Press.

Culler, Jonathan (1976). *Saussure*. Great Britain: Fontana/Collins.

Curtin, Philip D. (1969). *The Atlantic Slave Trade: A Census*. Madison, Wisconsin: The University of Wisconsin Press.

Dahrendorf, Ralf (1959). *Class and Class Conflict in Industrial Society*. Stanford, California: Stanford University Press.

Degler, Carl N. (1972). "Slavery and the Genesis of American Race Prejudice." In Donald Noel (Ed.), *The Origins of American Slavery and Racism* (pp. 59-80). Ohio: Charles E. Merrill Publishing Co.

DeMarco, Joseph P. (1983). *The Social Thought of W.E.B. Du Bois*. Lanham, MD: University Press of America.

Diop, Cheikh A. (1981). *Civilization or Barbarism: An Authentic Anthropology*. New York: Lawrence Hill Books.

Douglas, M. (1986). *How Institutions Think*. New York: Syracuse University Press.

Drake, St. Claire (1965). "The Social and Economic Status of the Negro in the United States." In Talcott Parsons and Kenneth B. Clark (Eds.), *The Negro American* (pp. 3-46). Boston: Houghton Mifflin Company.

Du Bois, W.E.B. (1995 [1903]). *The Souls of Black Folk*. New York: Penguin Putnam Inc.

Du Bois, W.E.B. (1984 [1940]). *Dusk of Dawn: An Essay toward an Autobiography of a Race Concept*. New Brunswick and London: Transaction Books.

Du Bois, W.E.B. (1971a [1897]). "The Conservation of Races." In Julius Lester (Ed.), *The Seventh Son: The Thought and Writings of W.E.B. Du Bois (Volume I)* (pp. 176-187). New York: Random House.

Du Bois, W.E.B. (1971b [1935]). "A Negro Nation Within The Nation." In Julius Lester (Ed.), *The Seventh Son: The Thought and Writings of W.E.B. Du Bois (Volume II)* (pp. 399-407). New York: Random House.

Du Bois, W.E.B. (1970 [1939]). *Black Folk, Then and Now: An Essay in the History and Sociology of the Negro Race*. New York: Octagon Books.

Du Bois, W. E. B. (1968). *The Autobiography of W.E.B. Du Bois: A Soliloquy on Viewing My Life from the Last Decade of its First Century*. US: International Publishers Co., Inc.

Du Bois, W.E.B. (1967 [1899]). *The Philadelphia Negro: A Social Study*. New York: Schocken Books.

Durkheim, Emile (1984 [1893]). *The Division of Labor in Society* (W.D. Halls, Trans.). New York: The Free Press.

Eagleton, Terry (1999). *Marx*. New York: Routledge.

Eagleton, Terry (1991). *Ideology: An Introduction*. London: Verso.

Early, Gerald (ed.) (1993). *Lure and Loathing: Essays on Race, Identity, and the Ambivalence of Assimilation*. New York: The Penguin Press.

Edgar, Andrew and Peter Sedgwick (Eds.) (1999). *Key Concepts in Cultural Theory*. London: Routledge.

Elkins, Stanley (1959). *Slavery: A Problem in American Institutional and Intellectual Life*. Chicago: University of Chicago Press.
Elkins, Stanley M. (1972). "The Dynamics of Unopposed Capitalism." In Donald Noel (Ed.), *The Origins of American Slavery and Racism* (pp. 45-58). Ohio: Charles E. Merrill Publishing Co.
Engels, Frederick (2000 [1884]. *The Origin of the Family, Private Property, and the State*. New York: Pathfinder Press.
Fanon, Frantz (1967). *Black Skin, White Masks* (Charles Lam Markmann, Trans.). New York: Grove Press.
Fanon, Frantz (1963). *The Wretched of the Earth* (Constance Farrington, Trans). New York: Grove Press.
Fogel, Robert W. (2003). *The Slavery Debates, 1952-1990: A Retrospective*. Baton Rouge: Louisiana State University Press.
Foner, Eric (1988). *Reconstruction: America's Unfinished Revolution 1863-1877.* New York: Harper&Row Publishers.
Foner, Eric (1990). *A Short History of Reconstruction 1863-1877.* New York Harper&Row Publishers.
Foucault, Michel (1977). *Discipline and Punish: The Birth of the Prison* (Alan Sheridan, Trans.). London: Penguin Books.
Franklin, John Hope and Alfred A. Moss Jr. (2000). *From Slavery to Freedom: A History of African Americans* (Eighth Edition). New York: Alfred A. Knopf.
Fraser, Nancy (1997). Justice *Interruptus: Critical Reflections on the "Postsocialist" Condition*. New York & London: Routledge.
Frazier, Franklin E. (1939). *The Negro Family in America*. Chicago: University of Chicago Press.
Frazier, Franklin E. (1957). *Black Bourgeoisie: The Rise of a New Middle Class*. New York: The Free Press.
Frazier, Franklin E. (1968). *The Free Negro Family*. New York: Arno Press and The New York Times.
Freud, Sigmund (1989 [1940]. *An Outline of Psycho-Analysis* (James Strachey, Trans. and Editor). New York: W.W. Norton & Company.
Freud, Sigmund (1989 [1921]. *Group Psychology and the Analysis of the Ego* (James Strachey, Trans. and Editor). New York: W.W. Norton & Company.
Freud, Sigmund (1989 [1917]. *Introductory Lectures on Psycho-Analysis* (James Strachey, Trans. and Editor). New York: W.W. Norton & Company.
Gadamer, Hans-Georg (2002). *Truth and Method* (Second, Revised Edition, Joel Weinsheimer and Donald G. Marshall, Trans.). New York: Continuum.
Gartman, David (2002). "Bourdieu's Theory of Cultural Change: Explication, Application, Critique." *Sociological Theory* 20 (2): 255-277.
Gates, Henry L. et al. (Eds.) (1997). *The Norton Anthology: African American Literature*. New York: W.W. Norton & Company inc.
Gates, Henry Louis, Jr. and Cornel West (1996). *The Future of the Race*. New York: Vintage Books.
Geertz, Clifford (1973). *The Interpretation of Cultures*. New York: Basic Books.

Geertz, Clifford (2000). *Local Knowledge: Further Essays in Interpretive Anthropology*. New York: Basic Books.
Genovese, Eugene (1974). *Roll, Jordan, Roll*. New York: Pantheon Books.
Geronimus, Arline T. and F. Phillip Thompson. "To Denigrate, Ignore, or Disrupt: Racial Inequality in Health and the Impact of a Policy-induced Breakdown of African American Communities." *Du Bois Review* 1; 2: 247-279.
Giddens, Anthony (1984). *The Constitution of Society: Outline of the Theory of Structuration*. Cambridge: Polity Press.
Gilroy, Paul (1993). *The Black Atlantic: Modernity and Double Consciousness*. Cambridge, Massachusetts: Harvard.
Glazer, Nathan and Daniel P. Moynihan (1963). *Beyond the Melting Pot*. Cambridge: Harvard University Press.
Gooding-Williams, Robert (1996). "Outlaw, Appiah, and Du Bois's "The Conservation of Races."" In Bell W. Bernard et al. (Eds.), *W.E.B. Du Bois on Race and Culture: Philosophy, Politics, and Poetics* (pp. 39-56). New York and London: Routledge.
Gramsci, Antonio (1959). *The Modern Prince, and Other Writings*. New York: International Publishers.
Grutter v. Bollinger et al, 539 U.S. 02-241 (2003); 13 (Slip Opinion).
Gutiérrez, Ramón A. (2004). "Internal Colonialism: An American Theory of Race." *Du Bois Review*, 1; 2: 281-295.
Gutman, Herbert (1976). *The Black Family in Slavery and Freedom 1750-1925*. New York: Pantheon Books.
Habermas, Jürgen (1987). *The Theory of Communicative Action: Lifeworld and System: A Critique of Functionalist Reason* (Volume 2, Thomas McCarthy, Trans.). Boston: Beacon Press.
Habermas, Jürgen (1984). *The Theory of Communicative Action: Reason and the Rationalization of Society* (Volume 1, Thomas McCarthy, Trans.). Boston: Beacon Press.
Handlin, Oscar and Mary F. Handlin (1972). "The Origins of Negro Slavery." In Donald Noel (Ed.), *The Origins of American Slavery and Racism* (pp. 21-44). Ohio: Charles E. Merrill Publishing Co.
Harding, Vincent (1981). *There is a River: The Black Struggle for Freedom in America*. New York: Harcourt Brace & Company.
Hare, Nathan (1991). *The Black Anglo-Saxons*. Chicago: Third World Press.
Harris, Marvin. (1999). *Theories of culture in postmodern times*. Walnut Creek, California: AltaMira Press.
Harris, David R. and Jeremiah Joseph Sim (2002). "Who is Multiracial? Assessing the Complexity of Lived Race." *American Sociological Review* 67; 4: 614-627.
Hegel, G.W.F. (1977 [1807]). *Phenomenology of Spirit* (A.V. Miller, Trans.). Oxford: Oxford University Press.
Heidegger, Martin (1962 [1927]). *Being and Time*. New York: HarperSanFrancisco.
Helle, H.J. and S.N. Eisenstadt (ed.) (1985). *Macro-Sociological Theory: Perspectives on Sociological Theory* (Volume 1). United Kingdom: J.W. Arrowsmith Ltd.

Helle, H.J. and S.N. Eisenstadt (ed.) (1985). *Micro-Sociological Theory: Perspectives on Sociological Theory* (Volume 2). United Kingdom: J.W. Arrowsmith Ltd.

Herskovits, Melville J. (1958 [1941]). *The Myth of the Negro Past.* Boston: Beacon Press.

Hochschild, Jennifer L. (1984). *The New American Dilemma: Liberal Democracy and School Desegregation.* New Haven: Yale University Press.

Hogue, Lawrence W. (1996). *Race, Modernity, Postmodernity: A look at the History and the Literatures of People of Color Since the 1960s.* Albany: State University of New York Press.

Holloway, Joseph E. (ed.) (1990a). *Africanisms in American Culture.* Bloomington and Indianapolis: Indiana University Press.

Holloway, Joseph E. (1990b). "The Origins of African-American Culture." In Joseph Holloway (Ed.), *Africanisms in American Culture* (19-33). Bloomington and Indianapolis: Indiana University Press.

Holt, Thomas (1990). "The Political Uses of Alienation: W.E.B. Du Bois on Politics, Race, and Culture, 1903-1940." *American Quarterly* 42 (2): 301-323.

Horkheimer, Max and Theodor W. Adorno (2000 [1944]. *Dialectic of Enlightenment* (John Cumming, Trans.). New York: Continuum.

Horne, Gerald (1986). *Black and Red: W.E.B. Du Bois and the Afro-American Response to the Cold War, 1944-1963.* New York: State University of New York Press.

House, James S. (1977). "The Three Faces of Social Psychology." *Sociometry* 40: 161-177.

House, James S. (1981). "Social Structure and Personality." In Morris Rosenberg and Ralph Turner (Eds.), *Sociological Perspectives on Social Psychology* (pp. 525–561). New York: Basic Books.

Hudson, Kenneth and Andrea Coukos (2005). "The Dark Side of the Protestant Ethic: A Comparative Analysis of Welfare Reform." *Sociological Theory* 23 (1): 1-24.

Hunton, Alphaeus w. (1970). "W.E.B. Du Bois: the meaning of his life." In John Henrik Clarke et al (Eds.), *Black Titan: W.E.B. Du Bois* (pp. 131-137). Boston: Beacon Press.

Inkeles, Alex (1959). "Personality and Social Structure." In Robert K. Merton, Leonard Broom, and Leonard S. Cottrell, Jr. (eds.), *Sociology Today* (pp. 249-276). New York: Basic Books.

Inkeles, Alex (1960). "Industrial man: The Relation of Status, Experience, and Value." *American Journal of Sociology* 66: 1-31.

Inkeles, Alex (1969). "Making Men Modern: On the causes and consequences of individual change in six developing countries." *American Journal of Sociology* 75: 208-225.

Jameson, Fredric and Masao Miyoshi (ed.). (1998). *The Cultures of Globalization.* Durham: Duke University Press.

Jones, G.S. (1971). *Outcast London: A Study in the Relationship Between Classes in Victorian Society.* Oxford: Clarendon Press.

Jordan, Winthrop D. (1972). "Modern Tensions and the Origins of American Slavery." In Donald Noel (Ed.), *The Origins of American Slavery and Racism* (pp. 81-94). Ohio: Charles E. Merrill Publishing Co.

Kardiner, Abram and Lionel Ovesey (1962 [1951]). *The Mark of Oppression: Explorations in the Personality of the American Negro*. Meridian Ed.

Karenga, Maulana (1993). *Introduction to Black Studies*. California: The University of Sankore Press.

Kellner, Douglas (2002). "Theorizing Globalization." *Sociological Theory*, 20:3, 285–305.

Kneller, George F. (1964). *Introduction to the Philosophy of Education*. New York: John Wiley & Sons, Inc.

Kuhn, Thomas S. (1996). *The Structure of Scientific Revolutions* (Third Edition). Chicago: The University of Chicago Press.

Laclau, Ernesto and Chantal Mouffe (1985). *Hegemony & Socialist Strategy: Towards a Radical Democratic Politics*. New York and London: Verso.

Lester, Julius (ed.) (1971). *The Seventh Son: The Thought and Writings of W.E.B. Du Bois (Volume I)*. New York: Random House.

Lester, Julius (ed.) (1971). *The Seventh Son: The Thought and Writings of W.E.B. Du Bois* (Volume II). New York: Random House.

Lewis, David Levering (1993). *W.E.B. Du Bois: Biography of a Race 1868-1919*. New York: Henry Holt and Company.

Levine, Lawrence W. (1977). *Black Culture and Black Consciousness: Afro-American Folk Thought from Slavery to Freedom*. New York: Oxford University Press.

Lévi-Strauss, Claude (1963). *Structural Anthropology* (Claire Jacobson and Brooke Schoepf, Trans.). New York: Basic Books.

Lincoln, Eric C. and Lawrence H. Mamiya (1990). *The Black Church in the African American Experience*. Durham and London: Duke University Press.

Luckmann, Thomas (Ed.) (1978). *Phenomenology and Sociology: Selected Readings*. New York: Penguin Books.

Lukács, Georg (1971). *History and Class Consciousness: Studies in Marxist Dialectics* (Rodney Livingstone, Trans.). Cambridge, Massachusetts: The MIT Press.

Lukács, Georg (2000). *A Defence of History and Class Consciousness: Tailism and the Dialectic* (Esther Leslie, Trans.). London and New York: Verso.

Luscombe, David (1997). *A History of Western Philosophy: Medieval Thought*. Oxford: Oxford University Press.

Lyman, Stanford M. (1997). *Postmodernism and a Sociology of the Absurd and Other Essays on the "Nouvelle Vague" in American Social Science*. Fayetteville: The University of Arkansas Press.

Lyman, Stanford M. and Arthur J. Vidich (1985). *American Sociology: Worldly Rejections of Religion and Their Directions*. New Haven and London: Yale University Press.

Lyman, Stanford M. (1972). *The Black American in Sociological Thought*. New York.

Mageo, Jeannette Marie (1998). *Theorizing Self in Samoa: Emotions, Genders, and Sexualities*. Ann Arbor: The University of Michigan Press.

Massey, D.S., and Denton, N.A. (1993). *American Apartheid: Segregation and the Making of the Underclass*. Cambridge, MA: Harvard University Press.

Marable, Manning (1986). *W.E.B. Du Bois: Black Radical Democrat*. Boston: Twayne Publishers.

Marcuse, Herbert (1964). *One-Dimensional Man.* Boston: Beacon Press.
Marcuse, Herbert (1974). *Eros and Civilization: A Philosophical Inquiry into Freud.* Boston: Beacon Press.
Marshall, Gordon (Ed.) (1998). *A Dictionary of Sociology* (Second edition). Oxford: Oxford University Press.
Marx, Karl and Friedrich Engels (1964). *The Communist Manifesto.* London, England: Penguin Books.
Marx, Karl (1992 [1867]). *Capital: A Critique of Political Economy* (Volume 1, Samuel Moore and Edward Aveling, Trans.). New York: International Publishers.
Marx, Karl (1998 [1845]). *The German Ideology.* New York: Prometheus Books.
Mason, Patrick L. (1996). "Race, Culture, and the Market." *Journal of Black Studies,* 26: 6, 782-808.
Mead, George Herbert (1978 [1910]). "What Social Objects Must Psychology Presuppose." In Thomas Luckmann (Ed.), *Phenomenology and Sociology: Selected Readings* (17-24). New York: Penguin Books.
Meier, August (1963). *Negro Thought in America, 1880-1915: Racial Ideologies in the Age of Booker T. Washington.* Ann Arbor: The University of Michigan Press.
Meier, August and Elliott M. Rudwick (1976 [1966]). *From Plantation to Ghetto; an Interpretive History of American Negroes.* New York: Hill and Wang.
Mocombe, Paul C. (2004). "Who Makes Race Matter in Post-Industrial Capitalist America?" *Race, Gender & Class* 11, 4: 30-47.
Moore, Jerry D. (1997). *Visions of Culture: An Introduction to Anthropological Theories and Theorists.* Walnut Creek, California: AltaMira Press.
Moynihan, Daniel P. (1965). *The Negro Family.* Washington, D.C.: Office of Planning and Research, US Department of Labor.
Murray, Charles (1984). *Losing Ground: American Social Policy 1950-1980.* New York: Basic Books.
Myrdal, Gunnar (1944). *An American Dilemma: The Negro Problem and Modern Democracy.* New York: Harper & Row Publishers.
Nash, Gary B. (1972). "Red, White and Black: The Origins of Racism in Colonial America." In Donald Noel (Ed.), *The Origins of American Slavery and Racism* (pp. 131-152). Ohio: Charles E. Merrill Publishing Co.
Nietzsche, Friedrich (1956). *The Birth of Tragedy* and *The Genealogy of Morals* (Francis Golffing, Trans.). New York: Anchor Books.
Nobles, Wade (1987). *African American Families: Issues, Ideas, and Insights.* Oakland: Black Family Institute.
Noel, Donald L. (Ed.) (1972). *The Origins of American Slavery and Racism.* Columbus, Ohio: Charles E. Merrill Publishing Co.
Noel, Donald L. (1972). "A Theory of the Origins of Ethnic Stratification." In Donald Noel (Ed.), *The Origins of American Slavery and Racism* (pp. 106-127). Ohio: Charles E. Merrill Publishing Co.
Noel, Donald L. (1972). "Slavery and the Rise of Racism." In Donald Noel (Ed.), *The Origins of American Slavery and Racism* (pp. 153-174). Ohio: Charles E. Merrill Publishing Co.

Obeyesekere, Gananath (1997 [1992]). *The Apotheosis of Captain Cook: European Mythmaking in the Pacific.* Hawaii: Bishop Museum Press.
Ortner, Sherry (1984). "Theory in Anthropology Since the Sixties," *Comparative Studies in Society and History* 26: 126-66.
Outlaw, Lucius (1996). "'Conserve' Races?: In Defense of W.E.B. Du Bois." In Bernard W. Bell et al (Eds.), *W.E.B. Du Bois on Race and Culture: Philosophy, Politics, and Poetics* (pp. 15-38). New York and London: Routledge.
Parsons, Talcott (1951). *The Social System.* Glencoe, Illinois: Free Press.
Parsons, Talcott (1954). *Essays in Sociological Theory.* Glencoe, Illinois: Free Press.
Parsons, Talcott (1977). *Social Systems and the Evolutions of Action Theory.* New York: Free Press.
Patterson, Orlando (1982). *Slavery and Social Death: A Comparative Study.* Cambridge, Massachusetts: Harvard University Press.
Phillips, U.B. (1918). *American Negro Slavery: A survey of the Supply, Employment, and Control of Negro Labor as Determined by the Plantation Regime.* New York: D. Appleton and Company.
Phillips, U.B. (1963). *Life and Labor in the Old South.* Boston: Little Brown.
Polanyi, Karl (2001 [1944]). *The Great Transformation: The Political and Economic Origins of Our Time.* Boston: Beacon Press.
Psathas, George (1989). *Phenomenology and Sociology: Theory and Research.* Washington, D.C.: University Press of America.
Rampersad, Arnold (1976). *The Art and Imagination of W.E.B. Du Bois.* Cambridge, Massachusetts: Harvard University Press.
Rao, Hayagreeva et al (2005). "Border Crossing: Bricolage and the Erosion of Categorical Boundaries in French Gastronomy," *American Sociological Review* 70: 968-991.
Reed, Adolph L. (1997). *W.E.B. Du Bois and American Political Thought: Fabianism and the Color Line.* New York and Oxford: Oxford University Press.
Reyna, Stephen P. (1997). "Theory in Anthropology in the Nineties," *Cultural Dynamics* 9 (3): 325-350.
Roediger, David R. (1999). *The Wages of Whiteness: Race and the Making of the American Working Class.* London and New York: Verso.
Rose, Sonya O. (1997). "Class Formation and the Quintessential Worker." In John R. Hall (Ed.), *Reworking Class* (pp. 133-166). Ithaca and London: Cornell University Press.
Rosenau, Pauline Marie (1992). *Post-Modernism and the Social Sciences: Insights, Inroads, and Intrusions.* Princeton, New Jersey: Princeton University Press.
Rubin, Vera (Ed.) (1960). *Caribbean Studies: A Symposium.* Seattle: University of Washington Press.
Sahlins, Marshall (1995a). *How "Natives" Think: About Captain Cook, For Example.* Chicago: University of Chicago Press.
Sahlins, Marshall (1995b). *Historical Metaphors and Mythical Realities.* Ann Arbor: University of Michigan Press.
Sahlins, Marshall (1990). "The Political Economy of Grandeur in Hawaii from 1810 1830." In Emiko Ohnuki-Tierney (Ed.), *Culture through Time: Anthropological Approaches* (pp. 26-56). California: Stanford University Press.

Sahlins, Marshall (1989). "Captain Cook at Hawaii," *The Journal of the Polynesian Society* 98; 4: 371-423.
Sahlins, Marshall (1985). *Islands of History*. Chicago: University of Chicago Press.
Sahlins, Marshall (1982). "The Apotheosis of Captain Cook." In Michel Izard and Pierre Smith (Eds.), *Between Belief and Transgression* (pp. 73–102). Chicago: University of Chicago Press.
Sahlins, Marshall (1976). *Culture and Practical Reason*. Chicago, IL: University of Chicago Press.
Said, Edward (1979). *Orientalism*. New York: Vintage Books.
Sarup, Madan (1993). *An Introductory Guide to Post-Structuralism and Postmodernism* (second edition). Athens: The University of Georgia Press.
Saussure de, Ferdinand (1972 [1916]. *Course in General Linguistics*, Edited by Charles Bally et al. Illinois: Open Court.
Schutz, Alfred (1978). "Phenomenology and the Social Sciences." In Thomas Luckmann (Ed.), *Phenomenology and Sociology: Selected Readings* (pp. 119–141). New York: Penguin Books.
Schutz, Alfred (1978). " Some Structures of the Life-World." In Thomas Luckmann (Ed.), *Phenomenology and Sociology: Selected Readings* (pp. 257–274). New York: Penguin Books.
Schwalbe, Michael L. (1993). "Goffman Against Postmodernism: Emotion and the Reality of the Self." *Symbolic Interaction* 16(4): 333-350.
Searle, John R. (1997). *The Mystery of Consciousness*. New York: The New York Review of Books.
Sennett, Richard (1998). *The Corrosion of Character*. New York: W.W. Norton & Company.
Sklair, Leslie (1995). *Sociology of the Global System*. Baltimore: Westview Press.
Skorupski, John (1993). *A History of Western Philosophy: English-Language Philosophy 1750-1945*. Oxford: Oxford University Press.
Slemon, Stephen (1995). "The Scramble for Post-colonialism." In Bill Ashcroft et al (Eds.), *The Post-colonial Studies Reader* (pp. 45-52). London and New York: Routledge.
Smedley, Audrey (1999). *Race in North America: Origin and Evolution of a Worldview* (Second edition). Boulder, Colorado: Westview Press.
Smiley Group, Inc. (2006). *The Covenant with Black America*. Chicago: Third World Press.
Smith M.G. (1960). "The African Heritage in the Caribbean." In Vera Rubin (Ed.), *Caribbean Studies: A Symposium* (pp. 34-46). Seattle: University of   W a s h - ington Press.
Solomon, Robert C. (1988). *A History of Western Philosophy: Continental Philosophy Since 1750, The Rise and Fall of the Self*. Oxford: Oxford University Press.
Sowell, Thomas (1975). *Race and Economics*. New York: David McKay.
Sowell, Thomas (1981). *Ethnic America*. New York: Basic Books.
Spivak, Chakravorty Gayatri (1994 [1988]). "Can the Subaltern Speak?" In Patrick Williams and Laura Chrisma (Eds.), *Colonial Discourse and Post-Colonial Theory A Reader* (pp. 66-111). New York: Columbia University Press.

Stack, Carol B. (1974). *All Our Kin: Strategies for Survival in a Black Community*. New York: Harper & Row Publishers.

Stampp, Kenneth (1967). *The Peculiar Institution*. New York: Alfred Knopf, Inc.

Staples, Robert (ed.) (1978). *The Black Family: Essays and Studies*. California: Wadsworth Publishing Company.

Stewart, David and Algis Mickunas (1990). *Exploring Phenomenology: A Guide to the Field and its Literature* (Second edition). Athens: Ohio University Press.

Strauss, Claudia and Naomi Quinn (1997). *A Cognitive Theory of Cultural Meaning*. United Kingdom: Cambridge University Press.

Stuckey, Sterling (1987). *Slave Culture: Nationalist Theory and the Foundations of Black America*. New York and Oxford: Oxford University Press.

Sturrock, John (ed.) (1979). *Structuralism and Since: From Lévi-Strauss to Derrida*. Oxford: Oxford University Press.

Sudarkasa, Niara (1980). "African and Afro-American Family Structure: A Comparison," The *Black Scholar*, 11: 37-60.

Sudarkasa, Niara (1981). "Interpreting the African Heritage in Afro-American Family Organization." In Harriette P. McAdoo (Ed.), *Black Families*. California: Sage Publications.

Sundquist, Eric J. (ed.) (1996). *The Oxford W.E.B. Du Bois Reader*. New York and Oxford: Oxford University Press.

Thomas, Nicholas (1982). "A Cultural Appropriation of History? Sahlins Among the Hawaiians," *Canberra Anthropology* 5; 1: 60-65.

Thompson, E.P. (1964). *The Making of the English Working Class*. New York: Pantheon Books.

Thompson, E.P. (1978). *The Poverty of Theory and Other Essays*. New York: Monthly Review Press.

Tulloch, Hugh (1999). *The Debate on the American Civil War Era*. Manchester: Manchester University Press.

Turner, Ralph H. (1976). "The Real Self: From Institution to Impulse." *American Journal of Sociology* 81: 989-1016.

Turner, Ralph H. (1988). "Personality in Society: Social Psychology's Contribution to Sociology." *Social Psychology Quarterly* 51; 1: 1-10.

Tussman, Joseph and Jacobus TenBroek (1949). "The Equal Protection of the Laws."*California Law Review* 37;3:341-381.

Wallerstein, Immanuel (1982). "The Rise and Future Demise of the World Capitalist System: Concepts for Comparative Analysis." In Hamza Alavi and Teodor Shanin (Eds.), *Introduction to the Sociology of "Developing Societies"* (pp. 29-53). New York: Monthly Review Press.

Ward, Glenn (1997). *Postmodernism*. London: Hodder & Stoughton Ltd.

Watkins, S. Craig (1998). *Representing: Hip-Hop Culture and the Production of Black Cinema*. Chicago: The University of Chicago Press.

Weber, Max (1958 [1904-1905]). *The Protestant Ethic and the Spirit of Capitalism* (Talcott Parsons, Trans.). New York: Charles Scribner's Sons.

West, Cornel (1993). *Race Matters*. New York: Vintage Books.

West, David (1996). *An Introduction to Continental Philosophy*. Cambridge: Polity Press.
Whipple, Mark (2005). "The Dewey-Lippmann Debate Today, Communication Distortions, Reflective Agency, and Participatory Democracy." *Sociological Theory*, 23 (2): 156-178.
Williams, Raymond (1977). *Marxism and Literature*. Oxford: Oxford University Press.
Wilson, Kirt H. (1999). "Towards a Discursive Theory of Racial Identity: The Souls of Black Folk as a Response to Nineteenth-Century Biological Determinism." *Western Journal of Communication*, 63 (2): 193-215.
Wilson, William J. (1978). *The Declining Significance of Race: Blacks and Changing American Institutions*. Chicago and London: The University of Chicago Press.
Wilson, William J. (1987). *The Truly Disadvantaged*. Chicago and London: University of Chicago Press.
Winant, Howard (2001). *The World is a Ghetto: Race and Democracy since World War II*. New York: Basic Books.
Wittgenstein, Ludwig (2001 [1953]). *Philosophical Investigations* (G.E.M. Anscombe Trans.). Malden, Massachusetts: Blackwell Publishers Ltd.
Wright, Kai (editor) (2001). *The African-American Archive: The History of the Black Experience in Documents*. New York: Black Dog & Leventhal Publishers.
Woodson, Carter G. (1969 [1933]). *The Mis-Education of the Negro*. Washington: Associated Publishers Inc.
Young, Iris Marion (1994). "Gender as Seriality: Thinking about Women as a Social Collective," *Signs* 19: 713-738.
Zamir, Shamoon (1995). *Dark Voices: W.E.B. Du Bois and American Thought, 1888-1903*. Chicago & London: The University of Chicago Press.
Zeitlin, Irving M. (1990). *Ideology and the development of sociological theory* (4th ed.). Englewood Cliffs, New Jersey: Prentice-Hall.

Index

acculturation, 35–37, 44nn24–26
Adorno, Theodor W. (1973 [1966]: 147), 66
Affirmative Action, 76
African American practical consciousness, constitution of: adopting singular practical consciousness, 22, 41n5; ambivalence of black bourgeoisie, 21, 22, 41n3; "class racism," 21, 33; class-color-caste system, development of, 35–37, 44n24, 72; discrimination, 22, 23; dominant social structure, 20, 60; Du Boisian double consciousness and, 60; identity construction in, 31–32; impact of slavery on, 71–72; liberal black (male) bourgeoisie and, 21, 41n2; ontological security and, 33, 35, 38, 43n20, 44n21; predestination, 31; protestant ethic and spirit of capitalism, 19; protestant ethic of society, 22, 31, 36, 71, 72; reproducing purposive-rationality, 36, 43n23; social actors/groups and, 20; structural variables and, 22
African cultural inheritance concept, 9, 15n2

African culture and black self-identity, 6–7
Africanism: retention of, 71; slave trade and, 22, 35; survival and, 7; W.E.B. DuBois on, 63, 68, 73
agency and consciousness: African American practical consciousness, 20, 41n1; black practical consciousness, 11–12, 29; capitalist social relations in, 10, 19; J̈rgen Habermas on, 11–12, 16n4; phenomenology, 10, 12; practical consciousness, 10, 12, 16n5, 19; structure, praxis and consciousness, 10–11. *See also* black American consciousness
Allen, Ernest Jr. (1992), 47, 79
Allen, Ernest Jr. (2002: 220), 49, 79
Allen, Ernest Jr. on Du Boisian double consciousness, 48–49
Allen, Richard L. (2001), 7, 19, 61, 79
Allen, Richard L. (2001: 30), 48
American Negro culture, dependency of, 7
American racial-capitalist social formation: black practical-consciousness and, 29; capital accumulation, 28; "mechanical" formation of, 28–29, 42n11;

permanent dialectic in, 29;
Protestant rationalization of, 28, 29, 30–31; purposive-rationality in, 28, 30, 36, 42n16; slave trade and, 29–30
American society, historical constitution of: capitalistic economic action, 24; economic distribution of material goods, 26; internal contradictions in, 27; Jürgen Habermas on, 26; predestination and, 25, 26, 27, 38; Protestant ethic and, 23–26, 27; purposive-rationality in, 24, 25, 26, 28, 36; spirit of capitalism in, 23, 25–26, 27; systems and social integration in, 24
Appiah, Anthony (1985), 47, 49, 79
Appiah, Anthony on W.E.B. DuBois, 4
Aptheker, Herbert (1964), 35, 37, 79
Archer, Margaret S. (1985:60), 12, 79
Asante, (1988, 1990), 8
Asante, Molefi Kete (1988, 1990), 7, 79

Baker, Houston A. Jr. (1972), 48
Balibar, Étienne (1991: 89), 26
Balibar, Étienne (1991: 207), 57
Balibar, Étienne and Immanuel Wallerstein, (1991 [1988], 40, 80
Balibar, Étienne and Immanuel Wallerstein, (1991: 107), 25, 80
Balibar, Étienne on "class racism," 27
being in the world, 32, 33, 48, 70, 76
Bell, Bernard W. (1985, 1996), 48, 80
Bell, Bernard W. (1996: 92), 67, 80
Bell, Bernard W. (1996: 96), 48, 80
Bell, Bernard W. (1996: 98), 62, 80
Bell, Bernard W. et al (1996), 62, 80
Bennett, Lerone (1982), 5, 35, 37, 80
Berger, (1967), 60
Bhabha, Homi, 50, 80
Billingsley, Andrew (1968, 1970, 1993), 7, 80

biological determinism, 1, 2, 7, 9
black American consciousness: adaptive-vitality understanding of, 9, 15, 19, 72; African culture and, 6–7; approaches to understanding of, 7–9; "black blood," 4, 5; dilemmas in theorizing about, 9–10; divergences of black life, 9, 15n3, 16n5; explanation of, 2; functionalization of, 5; ideal type analysis of, 12–14; inferiority, 6; legal regulations and, 61–62; liberal black (male) bourgeoisie and, 2, 14, 15, 15n1, 21, 29; as multiple and diverse, 61, 71; pathological-pathogenic understanding of, 7–8, 9, 16n6, 19; practical black consciousness, 14, 16n5, 29, 33, 42n12; Protestant solidarity, 40; self-identity, 3–4, 5; social integration, 21; sociohistorical understanding of, 3–4, 6, 12–14; structural understanding of, 40–41, 45n30; structural variables of society and, 22; structurationist/praxis understanding of, 10–11; white American consciousness and, 5, 6. *See also* agency and consciousness; Protestantism
black American self-identity, 3–6
black communism, 69, 70n7, 73
black nationalism, 36, 39
black practical consciousness: agency and consciousness, 11–12, 29; black Protestant bourgeoisie and, 39; "class racism" and, 14, 33, 71; in contemporary black America, 77–78; Du Boisian double consciousness and, 60, 71; ethos of, 73; liberal black (male) bourgeoisie, 2, 14, 15, 15n1, 21, 71; as multiple and diverse, 61, 71; Protestantism and, 12, 26, 29; W.E.B. DuBois and, 72–73. *See*

also African American practical consciousness, constitution of
black Protestant bourgeoisie: ambivalence of, 21, 41n3; emergence of, 38; origin of Du Boisian double consciousness, 39; practical consciousness of, 39
Blassingame, John W. (1972), 7, 8, 19, 35, 37, 80
Blassingame, John W. (1972: 3), 33
Blassingame, John W. (1972: 17), 33
Blassingame, John W. (1972: 39), 22
Blassingame, John W. (1972: 62-63), 35
Blassingame, John W. (1972: 63), 37
Bourdieu, Pierre 1990 ([1980]), 10, 81
Boxill, Bernard R. on W.E.B. DuBois, 4–5, 81
Bruce, Dickinson D. on Du Boisian double consciousness, 47, 81
Bruce, Dickson D., Jr. (1992), 17, 81

capitalistic economic action defined, 24
"class racism": African American practical consciousness, 14, 33; ambivalence of black bourgeois, 21; black bourgeoisie and, 2, 6, 39, 71; capitalist relations of production and, 27; justifying treatment of blacks, 38; W.E.B. DuBois on, 58
class-color-caste system, development of, 35–37, 44n24
Cohen, J. (2002), 19, 29, 81
"communicative action," 28, 29
Congressional Black Caucus, 76
contemporary black America: accepting structural (class) terms of society, 75; African ethos in, 74, 77, 78n2; ambivalence in, 73, 76; black double consciousness, 76–77; Black power era, results of, 74–75; black practical consciousness in, 77; black underclass of, 75–76; hip-hop culture, 76; hybridity in, 74, 78n1; integrationist movement in, 75; liberal black bourgeoisie, 73–74; Protestant ethic in, 76; salvation in, 77, 78; soul-less social structure, 77–78; spirit of capitalism and, 73, 76, 77; state ideological apparatuses, 73, 75
Cosby, Bill, 76
Crothers, Charles (2003), 10, 81
Crothers, Charles (2003: 3), 10
Crouch, Stanley (1993), 5, 47, 49, 76, 82

Delaney, Martin, 36
DeMarco, Joseph P. (1983), 5, 49, 82
discrimination, 15, 22, 23
divergences of black life, 9, 15n3, 16n5
Drake, St. Claire (1965: 3), 37, 82
Du Boisian double consciousness: adaptive-vitality and, 2, 15, 15n8, 21; ambivalence in, 2, 46, 51, 64, 68, 69n2; basis for, 4, 39, 40; black Protestant bourgeoisie and, 39; deconstructed from racial ideology, 68–69; as embodiment of Du Bois, 73; estrangement in, 17, 39, 58-59, 66; ideals and practices of, 14–15; interpretations of, 47; liberal black bourgeoisie ambivalence, 15, 21, 40–41, 58, 73; metaphoric genius of, 47–48; neo-Lamarckian social science and, 46, 49; positivist readings of, 47; practical consciousness and, 50, 60; purpose of, 1–2; purposive rationality in, 2, 58, 65–69; racial ideas influence, 3, 6; racialized bicultural black self-identity and, 5–6; reconciling Negro "twoness," 58, 60–61; reconsideration of, 49–51; reference to black American biculturalism, 59; reinterpretation

of, 2; self conscious manhood, 40, 58; traditional assimilationist/nationalist readings of, 47, 48; two theoretical consciousnesses compared, 14
Du Bois, W.E.B.: on absolute equality of races, 67; advice to black Americans, 69; on Africanism, 63, 68, 73; agent of Protestant ethic, 52, 65, 66; ambition to excel, 62, 63–64; ambivalence of, 57, 58, 64, 66, 69; on attaining self conscious men, 58; biography of, 51; black American consciousness, 58, 72–73; black communism and, 69, 70n7, 73; concept of blood and nation, 58; conception of "double consciousness," 57–58; early thoughts and actions of, 51–55; education of, 51, 53; on end of discrimination, 68; at Harvard University, 63–64; liberal pan-African bourgeois nationalism, 66–67, 70n5; on Negro "otherness," 53–54, 70n3; as "other," 65–66; purposive-rational of, 65–69; racial prejudice and, 52–53; reconciling Negro "twoness," 58, 60–61; self conscious manhood, 65; socialized through ideological apparatuses, 61–62; "Talented Tenth," 63, 64, 65, 68, 69, 73; theories of race, 62–63; understanding his "black identity," 57; upbringing of, 52; white Americanism, 56–57
Du Bois, W.E.B. (1940), 49
Du Bois, W.E.B. (1968: 75), 52, 82
Du Bois, W.E.B. (1968: 93), 52, 82
Du Bois, W.E.B. (1968: 112-113), 63, 82
Du Bois, W.E.B. (1968: 120), 54, 82
Du Bois, W.E.B. (1970), 77, 82
Du Bois, W.E.B. (1970 [1939]), 77, 82
Du Bois, W.E.B. (1971 [1897]: 179-183), 55–56, 82
Du Bois, W.E.B. (1971 [1897]: 182), 67, 82
Du Bois, W.E.B. (1971 [1897: 182-183), 57, 82
Du Bois, W.E.B. (1971 [1935]: 401), 68, 82
Du Bois, W.E.B. (1984 [1940]), 5, 82
Du Bois, W.E.B. (1984 [1940]: 97-101), 63, 82
Du Bois, W.E.B. (1984 [1968]: 32), 67, 82
Du Bois, W.E.B. (1986 [1968]: 108), 54, 82
Du Bois, W.E.B. (1986 [1968]: 123), 55, 82
Du Bois, W.E.B. (1986 [1968]: 169), 68, 82
Du Bois, W.E.B. (1995 [1903]), 5–6, 15, 82
Du Bois, W.E.B. (1995 [1903]; 1972 [1897]), 8, 82
Du Bois, W.E.B. (1997 [1921]: 41), 67
Du Bois, W.E.B. (1997 [1921]: 41-42), 68
Du Bois, W.E.B. (2003 [1920]: 42), 54
Du Bois, W.E.B. (2003 [1920]: 115; 1968), 49

Early, Gerald (1993), 7, 47, 82
Elkins, Stanley, (1959), 7, 19, 36, 83

Fanon, Frantz, (1967 [1952]), 15, 83
"fictive ethnicity," 2
Franklin, (1957), 37
Franklin, John Hope and Alfred A. Moss Jr. (2000), 35, 77, 83
Fraser, (1996), 11
Fraser, Nancy (1997), 28, 83
Frazier, Franklin E. (1939), 35, 36, 83
Frazier, Franklin E. (1939; 1957), 6
Frazier, Franklin E. (1939, 1957), 7

Frazier, Franklin E. (1939; 1957), 19
Frazier, Franklin E. 1939; 1957), 39
Frazier, Franklin E. (1957), 8, 14, 83
Frazier, Franklin E. (1966 [1939]), 7, 83
Friedland, (2002:384), 26

Garnet, Henry Highland, 36, 39
Gartman, David (2002: 257), 26, 83
Garvey, Marcus, 39, 59
Genovese, Eugene (1974), 7, 19, 35, 36, 84
Geronimus, Arline and F. Phillip Thompson (2004), 75, 84
Giddens, Anthony (1984), 10, 11, 84
Gilroy, Paul (1993), 9, 19, 48, 61, 84
Glazer, Nathan, 7
Glazer, Nathan and Daniel Patrick Moynihan, (1963: 53), 7, 84
Gooding-Williams, Robert (1996: 3), 5, 84
Gramsci, Anthonio, "two theoretical consciousnesses," 14, 84
Gutiérrez, Ramón (2004), 75
Gutman, Herbert (1976), 8, 19, 35, 37
Gutman, Herbert (1976: 103, 155), 38
Gutman, Herbert (1976: 260), 7
Gutman, Herbert (1976: 328), 34, 84

Habernas, Jürgen, (1987 [1981]), 12, 21, 84
Habernas, Jürgen, (1987 [1981]: 306), 25
Habernas, Jürgen, (1987 [1981]: 313), 25
Habernas, Jürgen, (1987 [1981], 1984 [1981]), 10, 11
Habernas, Jürgen on the spirit of capitalism, 25–26, 84
Harding, Vincent (1981), 35, 37, 38, 84
Harding, Vincent D. (1981) on African slavery, 34, 84
Hare, Nathan (1965 [1991]), 14
Hare, Nathan (1991), 8, 84

Herskovits, (1941), 60
Herskovits, Melville J. (1958 [1941]), 8, 9, 85
Holloway, Joseph E. (1990), 19, 60, 85
Holloway, Joseph E. (1990: 1), 9
Holt, Thomas (1990), 47, 84
Hooks, (1981, 1994), 14
Hudson, Kenneth and Andrew Coukos, (2002), 19
Hudson, Kenneth and Andrew Coukos, (2005), 29, 85
hybridity, 74, 78n1

"iron cage" thesis (of Weber), 28

Jackson, Jesse, 76
Jones, G. S. (1971), 19, 29, 85
Jordan, Winthrop D. (1972), 35, 85

Kardiner, Abram and Lionel Ovesey, (1962), 8, 86
Kardiner, Abram and Lionel Ovesey, (1962 [1951]), 14
Karenga, Maulana (1993), 7, 19, 30, 35, 37, 60, 86
Karenga, Maulana (1993: 121-122), 30
Karenga, Maulana (1993: 276), 6
Karenga, Maulana (1993: 277), 8
Karenga, Maulana (1993: 280), 7
Karenga, Maulana (1993: 282-283), 8
Karenga, Maulana on enslavement of Africans, 30

Lester, Julius (1971), 54, 86
Levine, (1977), 8, 9, 19
Levine, Lawrence W. (1977), 7, 86
Lewis, David Levering (1992: 281), 48
Lewis, David Levering (1992: 301), 47
Lewis, David Levering (1993), 7, 86
Lewis, David Levering on Du Boisian double consciousness, 47, 86

liberal black (male) bourgeoisie:
ambivalence of, 15, 21; black
practical consciousness, 2, 14, 15,
15n1, 21, 41n2; "class racism," 14;
contemporary black America and,
73–74; ideological domination of,
2, 15, 15n1, 21; Protestantism and,
6, 29
Liebow, (1967), 60
Lincoln, Eric C. and Lawrence H.
Mamiya, (1990), 7, 86
Loury, Glenn, 76

Marable, Manning (1986: 51), 65, 86
Marsalis, Winston, 76
Marshall, Gordon (1998: 534), 24–25, 87
Mason, Patrick L. (1996), 77, 87
Massey, D. S. and Denton, N. A. (1993), 75, 86
Meier, August (1959, 1963), 47
Meier, August (1963), 5, 49, 87
Meier, August (1963, 1966), 36
Meier, August and Elliot M. Rudwick, (1966 [1976]: 127), 36, 87
Mocombe, Paul (2004), 75, 87
Morris, William, 64
Moynihan, Daniel Patrick, (1965), 7, 19, 87
Murray, Charles (1984), 3, 60, 87
Myrdal, Gunnar (1944), 7, 60, 87

"Negro Nation within the Nation," W.E.B. DuBois, 69
Negro Thought in America, August Meier, 47, 87
Nobles, Wade (1987), 7, 87

"Of Our Spiritual Strivings," W.E.B. DuBois, 3, 5, 56
ontological security, 33, 35, 38, 43n20, 44n21
Ortner, Sherry (1984), 10, 87
Outlaw, Lucius on W.E.B. DuBois, 4, 88

Patterson, Orlando (1982: 38), 72, 88
Patterson, Orlando (1982: 38 & 46), 13, 88
Patterson, Orlando (1982: 38-42), 21, 88
Patterson, Orlando (1982: 46), 72, 88
Polanyi, Karl (2001), 25, 88
predestination: accumulation of
capital and, 21, 31; African
Americans and, 32; economic gain
as sign of, 26, 42n6; economic
organization and, 25; ontological
security and, 27; reifying
Protestant practical consciousness,
26, 42n8
Protestantism: affinity with purposive-
rationality, 25; black practical
consciousness and, 12, 13, 26, 29,
77–78; economic organization of
society, 25; historical constitution
of America and, 23–25; liberal
black bourgeois Protestantism, 6,
29; predestination, 26, 32, 38,
42n8; "racial class" gendered
values, 29; slavery and, 32; spirit
of capitalism, 23, 25–26
purposive-rationality: African
American practical consciousness
and, 36, 43n23; American society
and, 24, 25, 26, 28, 36; Du Boisian
double consciousness and, 2, 58,
65–69; Protestantism and, 25;
racial-capitalist social formation
and, 28, 30, 36, 42n16

racial "class-for-itself," 21
racial class social system. *See* class-
color-caste system, development of
racial ideas, 3, 6
racial inferiority, 1, 3, 6, 62
racialized bicultural black self-
identity, 5–6
Reed, Adolph (1992: 261), 48
Reed, Adolph (1997), 5, 39, 47, 49, 77, 88

Reed, Adolph (1997: 28), 53
Reed, Adolph (1997: 96), 48
Reed, Adolph (1997: 119-121), 46
Reed, Adolph (1997) analysis of Du Bois, 39–40, 88

Sahlins, Marshall (1976, 1995 [1984], 10, 89
Sahlins, Marshall (1995 [1981]), 10, 88
self conscious manhood, 40, 58, 65
Sharpton, Al, 76
slave trade: Africanism and, 22, 35, 71; American caste system, 35–38; black resistance to, 34–35; decline in import of native-born Africans, 22; delimiting American social structure, 32–33; impact of, 71; origins of, 31–32, 42n17; predestination and, 32; Protestant values, 29, 32, 33; slave population in America (1860), 38; slave/free Negro population (1790-1860), *23*; white Protestant Americanism and, 34–35
Slemon, Stephen (1995: 47), 60, 89
Smedley, Audrey (1999: 53), 29, 89
Smith, (1957: 36), 9
Smith, (1996), 27
Sowell, Thomas (1975, 1981), 61, 75, 89
Stack, Carol B. (1974), 7, 90
Stampp, Kenneth (1956), 35, 36
Stampp, Kenneth (1956, 1971), 7, 19
Staples, Robert (1978), 7, 90
Steele, Shelby, 76
Steele, Shelby (1990), 75
"Strivings of the Negro People," W.E.B. DuBois, 3
structural theory, 10–12
Stuckey, Sterling (1987), 36, 90
Sudarkasa, Niara (1981), 8, 9
Sundquist, Eric J. (1996: 16), 48, 90
"systematic labor," 33

The Concept of Self: A Study of Black Identity and Self-Esteem, Sundquist, Eric J., 48
"The Conservation of Races," W.E.B. DuBois, 3, 4
The Covenant with Black America, Tavis Smiley, 75, 89
The Philadelphia Negro, W.E.B. Du Bois, 39
The Slave Community, John Blassingame, 35
The Souls of Black Folks, W.E.B. DuBois: basis of "double consciousness," 4; concept of blood and nation, 58, 60; divided consciousness, 58; Du Bois's Americanism, 55; Kirt H. Wilson on, 3; race as biological/spiritual, 1–2; spiritual idealism and musical style, 55–56; use of double consciousness in, 15, 40, 46
Turner, Nat, 36
two theoretical consciousnesses, 66

Vesey, Denmark, 36

Washington, Booker T., 36, 39, 58–59
Watkins, S. Craig (1998), 77, 90
W.E.B. Du Bois and American Political Thought: Fabianism and the Color Line, Adolph Reed, 46
Weber, Max (1958), 19, 23
Weber, Max (1958 [1904-1905]), 12, 90
Weber, Max (1958) on Protestant ethic, 23–24
West and Gates, (1997), 7
West, Cornel (1993), 7, 61, 90
West, David (1996), 51, 91
white American consciousness, 5, 6
white nationalism, 38
white Protestant Americanism: Africanisms, 35–36; black American consciousness, 21; black emulation of, 37, 44nn24–26;

class-color-caste system, development of, 35–37, 44n24; justifying slavery, 34; racial class ideological foundation, 34; slave trade, 34–35
Wilson, (2000: 75), 13
Wilson, Kirt H. on W.E.B. DuBois, 3, 5
Wilson, William J. (1978; 1981), 75, 91
Wilson, William J. (1978, 1996), 19, 91
Winant, Howard (2001), 33, 91
Woodson, (1933), 14
Woodson, Carter G. (1969), 8, 91

www.ingramcontent.com/pod-product-compliance
Lightning Source LLC
Chambersburg PA
CBHW031554300426
44111CB00006BA/316